simply knit 2

The simply knit story continues with this second collection of handknitting patterns. Capturing the spirit of the design credo of Carol Lapin, simply knit's guiding force and design head, these garments exemplify the use of shape, form and color to create innovative, contemporary knitwear.

Lana Grossa yarns have been used exclusively throughout the collection. These yarns—"Merino Big," "Bingo," "Cashmere+," "Due Chine," "Inserto," and "Royal Tweed"—are basic, luxurious fibers of the highest quality. Their selection enhances each design and assures that your garment will be a pleasure to both knit and wear.

Simply Knit 2 is for enjoying—each and every design is easily knittable, eminently wearable, and has its own sense of fun.

yin & yang

kaleidoscope

every which way

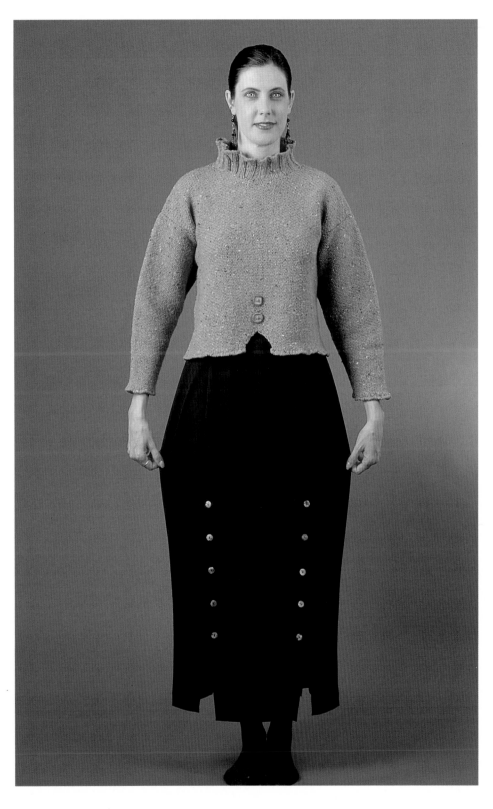

jolie

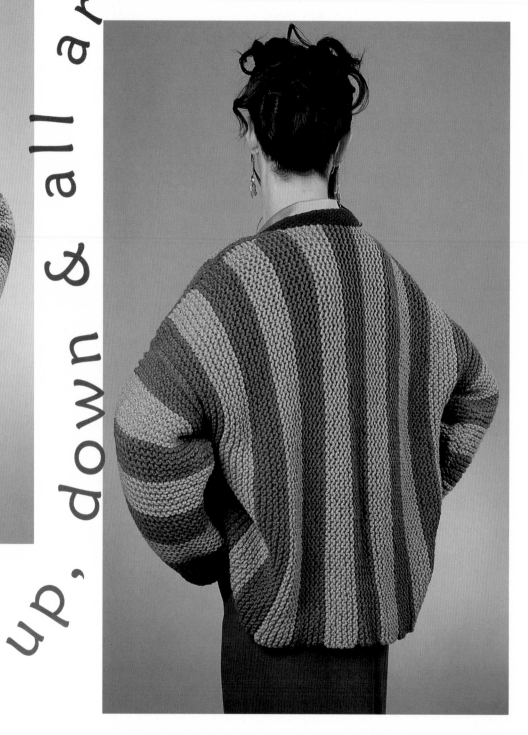

up, down & all around

ruffles & flourishes

prato

toscana

grey flannel jazz

waiting for godet

waiting for godet

baggy

simply scarves

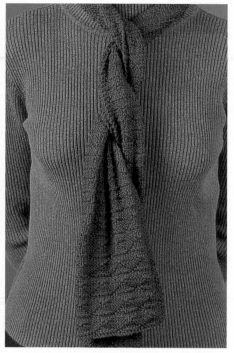

jester

lindy

claire

yin & yang

MATERIALS

YARN: LANA GROSSA "MERINO BIG" - 7 (8) SKEINS EACH OF COLOR A (#637) AND COLOR B (#618).
NEEDLES: US 7 (4.5 MM), OR CORRECT NEEDLE TO OBTAIN GAUGE.
ACCESSORIES: STITCH HOLDERS.

MEASUREMENTS

CHEST: 44 (50)".
LENGTH: 21 (22)".
SLEEVE LENGTH: 15½ (15½)".

GAUGE

ON US 7 IN ST ST: 20 STS AND 28 ROWS = 4".

FRONT A (RIGHT FRONT)
WITH US 7 AND COLOR A, CO 66 (74) STS.

ROW 1 (RS): KNIT.
ROW 2 (WS): PURL.
ROWS 3, 5, 7 AND 9 (RS): ([K2, P2 "RIB"] TO LAST 2 STS); END K2.
ROWS 4, 6, 8 AND 10 (WS): KNIT THE KNIT STS AND PURL THE PURL STS AS THEY FACE YOU.

ROW 11 (RS): RIB 20 STS, K46 (54).
ROW 12 (WS): KNIT THE KNIT STS AND PURL THE PURL STS AS THEY FACE YOU.

REP ROWS 11 AND 12 TWELVE MORE TIMES (26 ROWS TOTAL) (TO MODIFY LENGTH, SIMPLY ADD OR SUBTRACT REPS OF ROWS 11 AND 12).

NEXT ROW (RS): RIB 18, TURN AND LEAVE REM 48 (56) STS ON SPARE US 7 NEEDLE. WORK 8 MORE ROWS IN RIB ON THESE 18 STS, ENDING WITH WS FACING FOR NEXT ROW. PLACE STS ON HOLDER.

FRONT B (LEFT FRONT)
WITH US 7 AND COLOR B, CO 66 (74) STS.

ROW 1 (RS): KNIT.
ROW 2 (WS): PURL.
ROWS 3, 5, 7 AND 9 (RS): ([K2, P2] RIB TO LAST 2 STS); END K2.
ROWS 4, 6, 8 AND 10 (WS): KNIT THE KNIT STS AND PURL THE PURL STS AS THEY FACE YOU.

ROW 11 (RS): K46 (54), RIB 20 STS.
ROW 12 (WS): KNIT THE KNIT STS AND PURL THE PURL STS AS THEY FACE YOU.

REP ROWS 11 AND 12 TWELVE MORE TIMES (26 ROWS TOTAL) (OR TO MATCH FRONT A, IF LENGTH MODIFIED).

NEXT ROW (RS): REP ROW 11.

NEXT ROW (WS): RIB 18 STS, TURN AND LEAVE REM 48 (56) STS ON SPARE US 7 NEEDLE. WORK 8 MORE ROWS IN RIB ON THESE 18 STS, ENDING WITH RS FACING FOR NEXT ROW. PLACE STS ON HOLDER.

JOINING ROWS
(1) RIBBING B TO FRONT A
KEEPING 18 STS OF COLOR A ON HOLDER AT FRONT OF WORK, WITH COLOR B, RIB 18 STS OF FRONT B; ATTACH NEW COLOR A AND JOIN RIB TO FRONT A STS ON SPARE NEEDLE, WORKING P2, K46 (54) STS. BE SURE TO TWIST COLORS A AND B TOG TO AVOID HOLES. WORK THESE 66 (74) STS FOR 9 MORE ROWS AS SET, ENDING WITH RS FACING FOR NEXT ROW. REP FROM * TO *.

(2) RIBBING A TO FRONT B
WITH WS FACING, WORK 18 STS IN COLOR A FROM HOLDER AT FRONT OF WORK. JOIN TO FRONT B, WORKING K2, P46 (54) STS WITH COLOR B. WORK AN ADDITIONAL 9 ROWS AS SET, ENDING WITH WS FACING FOR NEXT ROW. REP FROM ** TO **. HOLD AT BACK OF WORK.

(3) RIBBING B TO FRONT B
WITH WS FACING, RIB 18 STS IN COLOR B FROM HOLDER, JOIN TO FRONT B BY WORKING K2, P46 (54) STS. WORK ANOTHER 9 ROWS AS SET, ENDING WITH WS FACING FOR NEXT ROW. REP FROM ** TO **. HOLD AT FRONT OF WORK.

(4) RIBBING A TO FRONT A
RETRIEVE THE 18 STS IN RIB IN COLOR A FROM HOLDER AT BACK OF WORK AND ON RS WORK IN COLOR A. JOIN TO FRONT A STS BY WORKING P2, K46 (54) STS FROM SPARE NEEDLE. WORK 9 MORE ROWS AS SET, ENDING WITH RS FACING FOR NEXT ROW. REP FROM * TO *.

REP (1) THROUGH (4), CROSSING A & B RIBBINGS ONCE MORE. FROM THEN ON, WORK EACH SIDE SEPARATELY.

AFTER WORKING 10 ROWS, DEC ON RS AS FOLLOWS: ON FRONT A, RIB 20 STS, SSK, KNIT TO END. ON FRONT B, K44 (56), K2TOG, RIB 20 STS. REP EVERY FOLLOWING 10TH ROW 5 TIMES (40 (48) STS ON NEEDLE). WHEN EACH SIDE MEASURES 21 (22)" FROM CO EDGE, PLACE 20 RIB STS ON SEPARATE HOLDERS. PLACE REM SHOULDER STS ON SEPARATE HOLDERS.

BACK
WITH US 7 AND COLOR B, CO 65 (73) STS. ON SAME NEEDLE AND COLOR A, CO 65 (73) STS. USING INTARSIA METHOD, CONTINUE AS FOLLOWS:

ROW 1 (RS): KNIT.

Row 2 (WS): Purl.

Rows 3, 5, 7 and 9 (RS): ([K2, p2 rib] to last 2 sts); end k2.

Rows 4, 6, 8 and 10 (WS): Knit the knit sts and purl the purl sts as they face you.

Row 11 (RS): K46 (54), ([p2, k2] 9 times), p2, k46 (54).

Row 12 (WS): Knit the knit sts and purl the purl sts as they face you.

Rep Rows 11 and 12 until piece measures 20 (21)" from CO edge.

Shape Back Neck

Work 48 (55) sts, BO next 34 (36) sts, work 48 (55) sts. Working each side separately, BO 3 (3) sts at neck edge twice, and 2 (1) st(s) once. Place rem 40 (48) sts on separate holders for shoulders.

Join Shoulders

With RS's facing, join shoulders using 3-needle bind-off method.

Neck

With RS facing, place 20 sts on holder for Front A onto US 7 and continue rib for 24 (26) rows. BO. With RS facing, place 20 sts on holder for Front B onto US 7 and continue rib for 24 (26) rows. BO. Sew pieces tog, then sew to back of neck.

Right Sleeve

With US 7 and Color B, CO 48 (52) sts.

Row 1 (RS): Knit.

Row 2 (WS): Purl.

Row 3 (RS): Change to Color A and knit.

Row 4 (WS): ([p2, k2] to end).

Row 5 (RS): Knit the knit sts and purl the purl sts as they face you.

Continue in st st, **AND AT SAME TIME**, inc 1 st at beg and end of next row, then every following 4th row, until there are 96 (100) sts on needle. Work without further shaping until piece measures 15½ (15½)" from CO edge. BO.

Left Sleeve

Work same as for right sleeve, casting on with Color A, and changing to Color B in Row 3.

Finishing

Center sleeves on shoulder seams and sew into place. Sew side and sleeve seams. Weave in ends behind front cable, being careful to avoid holes at point of color changes. Block to finished measurements.

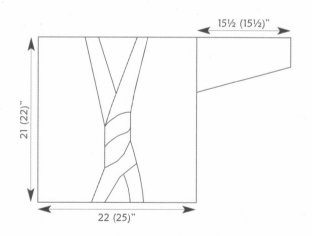

21 (22)"

15½ (15½)"

22 (25)"

kaleidoscope

MATERIALS

YARN: Lana Grossa "Merino Big" - 2 skeins each of #621, #628, #629 and #647; 3 skeins each of #626, #637, #640, #646 and 648; 6 skeins #623.

NEEDLES: Three 24" circular US 6 (4 mm), *or correct needle to obtain gauge.* 2 short double-pointed US 6 (4 mm).

ACCESSORIES: Stitch holders.

MEASUREMENTS

CHEST: 58".
LENGTH: 27".
SLEEVE LENGTH: 13½".

GAUGE

ON US 6 IN GARTER ST: 24 STS AND 48 ROWS = 4".

NOTES

Work jacket in 12 separate panels, then join by picking up sts along edges of adjacent panels and joining tog using 3-needle bind-off method. "Garter ridge" means 2 rows.

3-NEEDLE BIND-OFF METHOD

With WS's facing, hold needles parallel. *With 3rd needle, knit tog 1st st of needle 1 with 1st st of needle 2; knit tog 2nd st of needle 1 with 2nd st of needle 2; pass 1st st over 2nd st (BO)**; rep from * to ** until 1 st rems. Pull yarn through last rem st.

APPLIED CORDED EDGING

With short double-pointed US 6 and Color #623, CO 3 sts. With same needle, WS facing, *pick up 1 st; slide all 4 sts to opposite end of needle; k2, k2tog**; rep from * to **.

BACK

See **Back Chart** on page 9 for panel placement and color sequence.

PANELS 4, 6 AND 8

With US 6 and color indicated on chart, CO 34 sts. Following color sequence shown, work in garter st, slipping 1st st knitwise and purling last st on every row; **AND AT SAME TIME**, dec 1 st at beg and end of RS row after 4", 8", 12" and 16" as follows: sl1 knitwise, k2tog; knit to last 3 sts; k2tog, p1. Continue without further shaping until color sequence for panel is complete. BO.

PANELS 5, 7 AND 9

With US 6 and color indicated on chart, CO 34 sts. Following color sequence shown, work in garter st, slipping 1st st knitwise and purling last st on every row; **AND AT SAME TIME**, dec 1 st at beg and end of RS row after 3", 7", 11" and 15" as follows: sl1

kaleidoscope

knitwise, k2tog; knit to last 3 sts; k2tog, p1. Continue without further shaping until color sequence for panel is complete. BO.

Left Front
See **Left Front Chart** on page 8 for panel placement and color sequences.

Panel 10
Work same as for Panels 4, 6 and 8.

Panel 11
Work same as for Panels 5, 7 and 9.

Panel 12
With US 6 and color indicated on chart, CO 34 sts. Following color sequence shown, work in garter st, slipping 1st st knitwise and purling last st on every row; **AND AT SAME TIME,** dec 1 st at **BEG** of RS row every 2" 8 times as follows: sl1 knitwise, k2tog; knit to last st; p1. **AT SAME TIME,** when piece measures 12" (approx. 71 garter ridges), beg neck shaping:

Shape Neck
Dec 1 st at **END** of RS row every 6th garter ridge 15 times as follows: sl1 knitwise; knit to last 3 sts; k2tog, p1. Work on rem 11 sts without further shaping until color sequence for panel is complete. BO.

Right Front
See **Right Front Chart** on page 8 for panel placement and color sequences.

Panel 1
With US 6 and color indicated on chart, CO 34 sts. Following color sequence shown, work in garter st, slipping 1st st knitwise and purling last st on every row; **AND AT SAME TIME,** dec 1 st at **END** of RS row every 2" 8 times as follows: sl1 knitwise; knit to last 3 sts; k2tog, p1. **AT SAME TIME,** when piece measures 12" (approx. 71 garter ridges), beg neck shaping:

Shape Neck
Dec 1 st at **BEG** of RS row every 6th garter ridge 15 times as follows: sl1 knitwise, k2tog; knit to last st; p1. Work on rem 11 sts without further shaping until color sequence for panel is complete. BO.

Panel 2
Work same as for Panels 4, 6 and 8.

Panel 3
Work same as for Panels 5, 7 and 9.

Join Panels
See charts on page 8 and 9 for panel placement and bind-off color sequences.

With US 6 and color indicated, RS facing, pick up 158 sts along left edge of Panel 4. With another US 6 and same color, pick up 158 sts along right edge of Panel 5. With WS's facing, join tog using **3-Needle Bind-Off Method.**

Using **3-Needle Bind-Off Method** above, join Panel 5 to Panel 6, Panel 6 to Panel 7, Panel 7 to Panel 8 and Panel 8 to Panel 9 to complete back. Join Panel 1 to Panel 2 and Panel 2 to Panel 3 to complete right front. Join Panel 10 to Panel 11 and Panel 11 to Panel 12 to complete left front.

Join Shoulders
With US 6 and Color #626 (for right shoulder), or Color #628 (for left shoulder), RS facing, pick up 64 sts along each shoulder. With WS's facing, join using **3-Needle Bind-off Method.**

Sleeves (worked from shoulder to wrist)
With US 6 and Color #648 (for right sleeve), or Color #623 (for left sleeve), CO 121 sts. Following **Color Sequence for Sleeves** (opposite page), work in garter st, slipping 1st st knitwise and purling last st on every row, **AND AT SAME TIME,** dec 1 st at beg and end of every 4th garter ridge (8th row) in the following manner: sl1 knitwise, k2tog; knit to last 3 sts, k2tog, p1. When 82 sts rem, work without further shaping until sleeve measures 13½". BO.

Join Sleeves to Body
With US 6 and Color #637 (for right sleeve), or Color #646 (for left sleeve), RS's facing, pick up 121 sts along top of sleeve. With another US 6 and same color, pick up 60 sts along body to shoulder, 1 st in shoulder seam, and 60 sts from shoulder along body.

WITH WS'S FACING, JOIN USING **3-NEEDLE BIND-OFF METHOD**.

JOIN SIDE SEAMS

WITH US 6 AND COLOR #648, RS FACING, PICK UP 1 ST IN EACH GARTER RIDGE ALONG LEFT EDGE OF PANEL 3 UP TO SLEEVE. WITH ANOTHER US 6 AND SAME COLOR, RS'S FACING, PICK UP 1 ST IN EACH GARTER RIDGE ALONG RIGHT EDGE OF PANEL 4. WITH WS'S FACING, JOIN USING **3-NEEDLE BIND-OFF-METHOD**. JOIN PANEL 9 TO PANEL 10 IN THE SAME MANNER.

JOIN SLEEVE SEAMS

WITH US 6 AND COLOR #626 (FOR RIGHT SLEEVE), OR COLOR #640 (FOR LEFT SLEEVE), RS FACING, PICK UP 1 ST IN EACH GARTER RIDGE ALONG SLEEVE EDGE. WITH ANOTHER US 6 AND SAME COLOR, RS FACING, PICK UP 1 ST IN EACH GARTER RIDGE ALONG OTHER SLEEVE EDGE. WITH WS'S FACING, JOIN USING **3-NEEDLE BIND-OFF-METHOD**.

LEFT FRONT BORDER

WITH US 6 AND COLOR #623, CO 37 STS.

ROW 1 (RS): K18, SL1, K18.
ROW 2 (WS): PURL.
ROW 3 (RS): K4; *CO AND BO 4 STS IN NEXT ST; K3**; REP FROM * TO **; END K1, SL1, K18.
ROW 4 (WS): PURL.

ROW 5 (RS): K2; *CO AND BO 4 STS IN NEXT ST; K3**; REP FROM * TO **; END K3, SL1, K18.
ROW 6 (WS): PURL.

REP ROWS 3-6 UNTIL PIECE MEASURES APPROX. 31" (BORDER SHOULD FIT COMFORTABLY FROM BOTTOM OF JACKET TO CENTER OF BACK NECK).

RIGHT FRONT BORDER

WITH US 6 AND COLOR #623, CO 37 STS.

ROW 1 (RS): K18, SL1, K18.
ROW 2 (WS): PURL.
ROW 3 (RS): K18, SL1, K1; *CO AND BO 4 STS IN NEXT ST; K3**; REP FROM * TO **; END K4.
ROW 4 (WS): PURL.
ROW 5 (RS): K18, SL1; *K3; CO AND BO 4 STS IN NEXT ST; K3**; REP FROM * TO **; END K2.
ROW 6 (WS): PURL.

REP ROWS 3-6 UNTIL PIECE MEASURES APPROX. 31" (BORDER SHOULD FIT COMFORTABLY FROM BOTTOM OF JACKET TO CENTER OF BACK NECK).

FINISHING

JOIN RIGHT FRONT BORDER AND LEFT FRONT BORDER TO JACKET USING **3-NEEDLE BIND-OFF METHOD** OR SEW IF YOU PREFER. TURN FACING TO INSIDE ALONG SLIP ST AND SEW TO INSIDE. WORK **APPLIED CORDED EDGING** ALONG BOTTOM OF JACKET.

COLOR SEQUENCE FOR LEFT SLEEVE (FROM TOP DOWN)

10 GARTER RIDGES #623	10 GARTER RIDGES #646
5 GARTER RIDGES #621	4 GARTER RIDGES #629
13 GARTER RIDGES #626	8 GARTER RIDGES #647
8 GARTER RIDGES #640	10 GARTER RIDGES #648
6 GARTER RIDGES #637	3 GARTER RIDGES #628

COLOR SEQUENCE FOR RIGHT SLEEVE (FROM TOP DOWN)

8 GARTER RIDGES #648	12 GARTER RIDGES #640
12 GARTER RIDGES #637	9 GARTER RIDGES #626
8 GARTER RIDGES #646	4 GARTER RIDGES #623
5 GARTER RIDGES #629	6 GARTER RIDGES #637
6 GARTER RIDGES #647	7 GARTER RIDGES #646

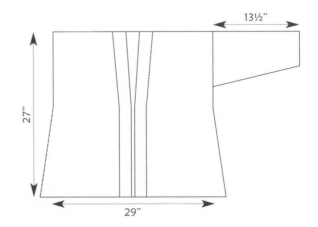

kaleidoscope

RIGHT FRONT

3	2	1
11 garter ridges #623	8 garter ridges #628	6 garter ridges #623
		4 garter ridges #646
	6 garter ridges #648	7 garter ridges #647
10 garter ridges #621		5 garter ridges #621
	12 garter ridges #629	
8 garter ridges #637		11 garter ridges #626
6 garter ridges #628	9 garter ridges #640	
		10 garter ridges #628
14 garter ridges #640	11 garter ridges #647	
		8 garter ridges #637
	5 garter ridges #626	
10 garter ridges #629		6 garter ridges #640
	15 garter ridges #637	
8 garter ridges #626		8 garter ridges #647
5 garter ridges #628	8 garter ridges #623	10 garter ridges #648
13 garter ridges #647	11 garter ridges #621	13 garter ridges #629
8 garter ridges #648	9 garter ridges #640	7 garter ridges #646
6 garter ridges #637	7 garter ridges #628	10 garter ridges #623
12 garter ridges #621	14 garter ridges #646	6 garter ridges #640
7 garter ridges #626	7 garter ridges #637	14 garter ridges #626
12 garter ridges #640	8 garter ridges #629	10 garter ridges #621
9 garter ridges #623	13 garter ridges #648	7 garter ridges #637
6 garter ridges #629	9 garter ridges #626	15 garter ridges #628
12 garter ridges #646	5 garter ridges #647	
CO WITH #646	CO WITH #647	CO WITH #628
3	**2**	**1**
USE #648 FOR SEAM	USE #628 FOR SEAM	USE #621 FOR SEAM

LEFT FRONT

12	1	10
13 garter ridges #648	6 garter ridges #629	8 garter ridges #626
	12 garter ridges #623	7 garter ridges #647
8 garter ridges #637		5 garter ridges #637
4 garter ridges #621	8 garter ridges #626	
		10 garter ridges #629
9 garter ridges #646	10 garter ridges #648	
		6 garter ridges #640
7 garter ridges #640	5 garter ridges #646	
	6 garter ridges #621	10 garter ridges #628
10 garter ridges #623		
	12 garter ridges #637	12 garter ridges #621
5 garter ridges #629		
9 garter ridges #626	9 garter ridges #628	10 garter ridges #648
6 garter ridges #647	7 garter ridges #640	7 garter ridges #646
9 garter ridges #648	10 garter ridges #647	13 garter ridges #623
13 garter ridges #621	7 garter ridges #629	6 garter ridges #637
6 garter ridges #628	13 garter ridges #626	11 garter ridges #640
8 garter ridges #646		
10 garter ridges #640	6 garter ridges #648	9 garter ridges #626
	11 garter ridges #621	5 garter ridges #647
6 garter ridges #637		11 garter ridges #646
15 garter ridges #623	8 garter ridges #628	
	6 garter ridges #640	8 garter ridges #629
7 garter ridges #626	14 garter ridges #646	6 garter ridges #628
12 garter ridges #629	7 garter ridges #637	13 garter ridges #648
CO WITH #629	CO WITH #637	CO WITH #648
12	**1**	**10**
USE #628 FOR SEAM	USE #640 FOR SEAM	USE #648 FOR SEAM

BACK

Column 9 — CO WITH #623 — USE #648 FOR SEAM

- 7 GARTER RIDGES #621
- 11 GARTER RIDGES #646
- 6 GARTER RIDGES #648
- 14 GARTER RIDGES #623
- 6 GARTER RIDGES #626
- 8 GARTER RIDGES #629
- 11 GARTER RIDGES #640
- 5 GARTER RIDGES #647
- 15 GARTER RIDGES #621
- 8 GARTER RIDGES #648
- 11 GARTER RIDGES #626
- 5 GARTER RIDGES #629
- 15 GARTER RIDGES #628
- 7 GARTER RIDGES #640
- 12 GARTER RIDGES #646
- 7 GARTER RIDGES #637
- 9 GARTER RIDGES #623

Column 8 — CO WITH #621 — USE #629 FOR SEAM

- 16 GARTER RIDGES #640
- 9 GARTER RIDGES #647
- 7 GARTER RIDGES #629
- 13 GARTER RIDGES #648
- 10 GARTER RIDGES #637
- 8 GARTER RIDGES #628
- 4 GARTER RIDGES #647
- 5 GARTER RIDGES #640
- 8 GARTER RIDGES #626
- 15 GARTER RIDGES #623
- 7 GARTER RIDGES #637
- 11 GARTER RIDGES #621
- 9 GARTER RIDGES #648
- 5 GARTER RIDGES #646
- 13 GARTER RIDGES #628
- 8 GARTER RIDGES #626
- 9 GARTER RIDGES #621

Column 7 — CO WITH #648 — USE #637 FOR SEAM

- 14 GARTER RIDGES #637
- 9 GARTER RIDGES #646
- 14 GARTER RIDGES #628
- 6 GARTER RIDGES #629
- 5 GARTER RIDGES #640
- 9 GARTER RIDGES #626
- 14 GARTER RIDGES #621
- 11 GARTER RIDGES #648
- 7 GARTER RIDGES #628
- 12 GARTER RIDGES #646
- 9 GARTER RIDGES #623
- 11 GARTER RIDGES #640
- 6 GARTER RIDGES #637
- 7 GARTER RIDGES #629
- 10 GARTER RIDGES #647
- 13 GARTER RIDGES #648

Column 6 — CO WITH #646 — USE #623 FOR SEAM

- 10 GARTER RIDGES #626
- 5 GARTER RIDGES #647
- 9 GARTER RIDGES #640
- 5 GARTER RIDGES #621
- 7 GARTER RIDGES #646
- 13 GARTER RIDGES #637
- 10 GARTER RIDGES #648
- 8 GARTER RIDGES #623
- 12 GARTER RIDGES #629
- 7 GARTER RIDGES #640
- 11 GARTER RIDGES #647
- 14 GARTER RIDGES #626
- 11 GARTER RIDGES #621
- 8 GARTER RIDGES #648
- 6 GARTER RIDGES #628
- 13 GARTER RIDGES #637
- 8 GARTER RIDGES #646

Column 5 — CO WITH #626 — USE #646 FOR SEAM

- 10 GARTER RIDGES #648
- 11 GARTER RIDGES #629
- 9 GARTER RIDGES #640
- 7 GARTER RIDGES #623
- 5 GARTER RIDGES #626
- 13 GARTER RIDGES #621
- 9 GARTER RIDGES #647
- 11 GARTER RIDGES #648
- 7 GARTER RIDGES #623
- 11 GARTER RIDGES #637
- 16 GARTER RIDGES #628
- 13 GARTER RIDGES #646
- 6 GARTER RIDGES #629
- 8 GARTER RIDGES #640
- 11 GARTER RIDGES #626

Column 4 — CO WITH #647 — USE #648 FOR SEAM

- 11 GARTER RIDGES #647
- 6 GARTER RIDGES #640
- 8 GARTER RIDGES #626
- 14 GARTER RIDGES #623
- 7 GARTER RIDGES #629
- 11 GARTER RIDGES #648
- 8 GARTER RIDGES #637
- 6 GARTER RIDGES #646
- 8 GARTER RIDGES #628
- 12 GARTER RIDGES #640
- 8 GARTER RIDGES #629
- 11 GARTER RIDGES #623
- 6 GARTER RIDGES #626
- 11 GARTER RIDGES #637
- 6 GARTER RIDGES #648
- 10 GARTER RIDGES #621
- 14 GARTER RIDGES #647

every which way

SEED STITCH
ROW 1 (RS): *K1, P1**; REP FROM * TO **.
ROW 2 (WS): PURL THE KNIT STS AND KNIT THE PURL STS AS THEY FACE YOU.

NOTE
STUDY SCHEMATIC ON PAGE 13 CAREFULLY.

LOWER RIGHT BACK (1)
WITH US 8 AND MC, CO 44 STS. WORK IN SEED STITCH FOR 2 ROWS. CHANGE TO CC AND WORK IN ST ST, ALTERNATING CC WITH MC EVERY 2 ROWS. CONTINUE AS SET UNTIL PIECE MEASURES 10½ (11½, 12½)" FROM CO EDGE, ENDING AFTER WORKING A RS MC ROW.

NEXT ROW (WS): WITH MC, WORK IN SEED STITCH. BO IN SEED STITCH.

LOWER LEFT BACK (2)
WORK AS FOR LOWER RIGHT BACK UNTIL BEFORE FINAL CC STRIPE.

MAKE BUTTONHOLES
NEXT ROW (RS): WITH CC, K4, ([YO, K2TOG, K7] 4 TIMES); YO, K2TOG, K2.
NEXT ROW (WS): WITH CC, PURL.

WORK LAST 2 ROWS WITH MC AS FOLLOWS: KNIT ON RS; WORK IN SEED STITCH ON WS. BO IN SEED STITCH.

UPPER BACK (3)
WITH US 6 AND MC, RS FACING, BEG AT CO EDGE, PICK UP 51 (55, 59) STS ALONG UPPER EDGE OF LOWER RIGHT BACK. BREAK YARN AND SET ASIDE.

WITH US 8 AND MC, RS FACING, BEG AT BO EDGE, PICK UP 51 (55, 59) STS ALONG UPPER EDGE OF LOWER LEFT BACK. TURN AND WORK SEED STITCH TO LAST 5 STS.

MATERIALS
YARN: LANA GROSSA "BINGO CHINE" - 8 (8, 9) SKEINS MC (#506); 7 (7, 8) SKEINS CC (#501).
NEEDLES: US 6 (4 MM) & US 8 (5 MM), *OR CORRECT NEEDLES TO OBTAIN GAUGE.*
ACCESSORIES: EIGHT ½" BUTTONS.

MEASUREMENTS
CHEST: 44 (48, 52)".
LENGTH: 22 (22, 22)".
SLEEVE LENGTH: 17 (17, 17)".

GAUGE
ON US 8 IN ST ST: 16 STS AND 22 ROWS = 4".

Join Lower Left Back & Lower Right Back

With WS facing, holding Lower Left Back behind Lower Right Back, and maintaining **Seed Stitch**, work last five sts from Lower Left Back tog with first five sts from Lower Right Back. With US 8, work rem sts of Lower Right Back in **Seed Stitch**. Work 2 more rows in **Seed Stitch**.

Change to CC and work in st st, alternating 4 rows of CC with 4 rows of MC. Continue until Upper Back measures 10½ (10½, 10½)", ending with RS facing for next row.

Shape Back Neck

Next Row (RS): K36 (40, 44) sts, BO next 25 (25, 25) sts, knit to end of row.

Working each side separately, work 1 WS row, then BO 2 sts at neck edge on next RS row, then work 1 more WS row. Place rem 34 (38, 42) shoulder sts on holder.

Lower Left Front (4)

With US 8 and MC, CO 32 sts. Work as for Lower Right Back until piece measures 10¼(11¼, 12¼)" from CO edge, ending after working 2 rows of CC. BO.

Lower Right Front (5)

With MC and larger needle, CO 32 sts and work as for Lower Left Back until piece measures 10¼(11¼, 12¼)", ending after working 2 rows of MC.

Next row (RS): With CC, knit.
Next row (WS) (Make Buttonholes): P2, ([yo, p2tog, p11] twice); yo, p2tog, p2. BO.

Upper Left Front (6)

With US 8 and MC, RS facing, beg at seed stitch edge, pick up 48 (52, 56) sts along upper side of Lower Left Front. Work in **Seed Stitch** for 3 rows.

Change to CC and work in st st, alternating 4 rows of CC with 4 rows of MC; **AND AT SAME TIME**, dec 1 st at neck edge on every 4th row 14 times. Work without further shaping on rem (34 (38, 42) sts until piece is same length as Upper Back. Place sts on holder.

Upper Right Front (7)

With US 8 and MC, RS facing, beg at buttonhole edge, pick up 48 (52, 56) sts along upper side of Lower Right Front. Work in **Seed Stitch** for 3 rows.

Change to CC and work in st st, alternating 4 rows of CC with 4 rows of MC; **AND AT SAME TIME**, dec 1 st at neck edge on every 4th row 14 times. Work without further shaping on rem 34 (38, 42) sts until piece is same length as Upper Left Front.

Join Shoulders

With RS's facing, join shoulders using 3-needle bind-off method.

Sleeves

With US 8 and MC, RS facing, pick up 48 (48, 48) sts between just above seed stitch band and shoulder seam and 48 (48, 48) sts from shoulder seam to just above seed stitch band.

Work in **Seed Stitch** for 3 rows.

Change to CC and work in st st, alternating 2 rows of CC with 2 rows of MC; **AND AT SAME TIME**, dec 1 st at beg and end of every 4th row 24 times (48 (48, 48) sts rem), ending with RS facing for next row. With MC, knit 1 RS row, then work in **Seed Stitch** for 2 rows. BO in **Seed Stitch**.

Lower Back Borders

With US 8 and MC, RS facing, pick up and knit 48 (52, 56) sts along bottom edge of Lower Left Back. Work in **Seed Stitch** for 2 rows. BO in **Seed Stitch**. Rep for Lower Right Back.

Lower Left Front Border (8)

With US 8 and MC, RS facing, pick up 48 (52, 56) sts along bottom edge of Lower Left Front. Work in **Seed Stitch** for 3 rows.

Row 4 (RS): With CC, k45 (49, 53); with MC k1, p1, k1.
Row 5 (WS): With MC, k1, p1, k1; with CC, purl to end of row.
Row 6 (RS): Rep Row 4.

Row 7 (WS): Rep Row 5.
Row 8 (RS): With MC, k46 (50, 54), p1, k1.
Row 9 (WS): With MC, k1, p1, k1; purl to end of row.
Row 10 (RS): Rep Row 8.
Row 11 (WS): Rep Row 9.
Rows 12-15: Rep Rows 4-7.
Row 16 (RS): Rep Row 8.

Work in **Seed Stitch** for 2 rows. BO in **Seed Stitch**.

Lower Right Front Border (9)
With US 8 and MC, RS facing, pick up 48 (52, 56) sts along bottom edge of Lower Right Front. Work 3 rows in **Seed Stitch**.

Row 4 (RS): With MC k1, p1, k1; with CC, knit to end of row.
Row 5 (WS): With CC, p45 (49, 53); with MC, k1, p1, k1.
Row 6 (RS): Rep Row 4.
Row 7 (WS): Rep Row 5.
Row 8 (RS): With MC, k1, p1; knit to end of row.
Row 9 (WS): With MC, p45 (49, 53) k1, p1, k1.
Row 10 (RS): Rep Row 8.
Row 11 (WS): Rep Row 9.
Rows 12-15: Rep Rows 4-7.
Row 16 (RS): Rep Row 8.

Work in **Seed Stitch** for 2 rows. BO in **Seed Stitch**.

Finishing
Sew side seams, leaving 4" open at bottom. Sew sleeve seams.

Neck and Front Border
With US 6 and MC, RS facing, pick up 15 (15, 15) sts up Lower Right Front border, 30 (30, 30) sts up Lower Right Front, 49 (49, 49) sts up Upper Right Front neck edge, 35 (35, 35) sts along back neck edge, 49 (49, 49) sts down Upper Left Front neck edge, 30 (30, 30) sts down Lower Left Front, 15 (15, 15) sts down Lower Left Front border (223 (223, 223) sts on needle). Work in **Seed Stitch** for 3 rows. BO in **Seed Stitch**.

Sew 5 buttons to Lower Right Back opposite buttonholes. Sew 3 buttons to Lower Left Front opposite buttonholes. Weave in ends. Block to finished measurements.

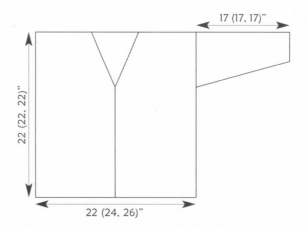

Back

Front

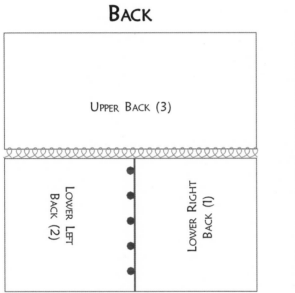

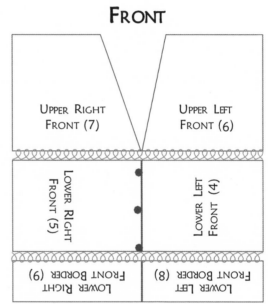

Back

Upper Back (3)

Lower Left Back (2)

Lower Right Back (1)

Front

Upper Right Front (7)

Upper Left Front (6)

Lower Right Front (5)

Lower Left Front (4)

Lower Right Front Border (9)

Lower Left Front Border (8)

Finishing Key

Pick up sts along edge.

jolie

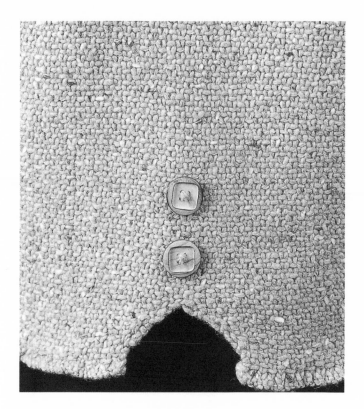

Materials

Yarn: Lana Grossa "Royal Tweed" - 8 (9, 10) skeins.
Shown in #13.
Needles: US 8 (5 mm) and US 13 (9 mm), *or correct needles to obtain gauge.*
Accessories: Two 1" buttons (optional).

Measurements

Chest: 40 (44, 48)".
Length: 20 (20, 20)".
Sleeve Length: 17 (17, 18)".

Gauge

On US 13 in Woven Stitch: 17 sts and 30 rows =4"

Woven Stitch

Row 1 (RS): *K1, sl1wyif**; rep from * to **.
Row 2 (WS): *P1, sl1wyib**; rep from * to **.

Rep Rows 1 and 2.

Back

With US 8, CO 176 (192, 208) sts.

Row 1 (RS): Knit.
Row 2 (WS): P2tog across row (88 (96, 104) sts rem).

Change to US 13 and work in Woven Stitch until piece measures 11 (11, 11)" from CO edge, ending with RS facing for next row.

Shape Armhole

BO 6 (6, 7) sts at beg of next 2 rows (76 (84, 90) sts rem), then continue in pattern until piece measures 19½ (19½, 20)" from CO edge, ending with RS facing for next row.

Shape Neck

Work 27 (31, 33) sts, BO next 22 (22, 24) sts, work 27 (31, 33) sts. Working each side separately, dec 1 st at neck edge once. Work 2 rows without further shaping. BO rem 26 (30, 32) shoulder sts.

Front

With US 8, CO 74 (82, 90) sts. Attach another ball of yarn and CO 74 (82, 90) more sts. Work both pieces with separate balls of yarn on same needle as follows:

Row 1 (RS): Knit.
Row 2 (WS): P2tog across row of first piece (37 (41, 45) sts rem); p2tog across row of 2nd piece (37, 41, 45) sts rem).

CHANGE TO US 13 AND CONTINUE WORKING PIECES SEPARATELY IN **WOVEN STITCH**, **AND AT SAME TIME**, INC 1 ST AT END OF FIRST PIECE AND 1 ST AT BEG OF 2ND PIECE ON EVERY RS ROW 7 TIMES (44 (48, 52) STS REM ON EACH PIECE), ENDING WITH RS FACING FOR NEXT ROW.

JOIN PIECES

NEXT ROW (RS): JOIN PIECES TOG BY WORKING ACROSS BOTH PIECES IN PATTERN (88 (96, 104) STS ON NEEDLE). CONTINUE IN PATTERN UNTIL PIECE MEASURES 11 (11, 11)" FROM CO EDGE, ENDING WITH RS FACING FOR NEXT ROW.

SHAPE ARMHOLE

BO 6 (6, 7) STS AT BEG OF NEXT 2 ROWS (76 (84, 90) STS REM). WORK WITHOUT FURTHER SHAPING UNTIL PIECE MEASURES 17 (17, 17½)" FROM CO EDGE, ENDING WITH RS FACING FOR NEXT ROW.

SHAPE NECK

WORK 35 (39, 41) STS, BO NEXT 6 (6, 8) STS, WORK 35 (39, 41) STS. WORKING EACH SIDE SEPARATELY, BO 2 STS AT NECK EDGE ONCE, THEN DEC 1 ST AT NECK EDGE EVERY OTHER ROW 7 TIMES. WORK WITHOUT FURTHER SHAPING UNTIL PIECE MEASURES SAME AS BACK. BO REM 26 (30, 32) SHOULDER STS.

SLEEVES

WITH US 8, CO 76 (76, 80) STS.

ROW 1 (RS): KNIT.
ROW 2 (WS): P2TOG ACROSS ROW (38 (38, 40) STS REM).

CHANGE TO US 13 AND WORK IN **WOVEN STITCH**, **AND AT SAME TIME**, INC 1 ST AT BEG AND END OF EVERY 4TH ROW UNTIL THERE ARE 84 (84, 88) STS ON NEEDLE. WORK WITHOUT FURTHER SHAPING UNTIL PIECE MEASURES 17 (17, 18)" FROM CO EDGE. BO.

FINISHING

SEW SHOULDERS TOG.

NECK

WITH CIRCULAR US 8, RS FACING, BEG AT RIGHT SHOULDER SEAM, PICK UP 34 (34, 34) STS ALONG BACK NECK EDGE, 17 (17, 17) DOWN LEFT NECK EDGE, 12 (12, 12) ALONG FRONT NECK EDGE, AND 17 (17, 17) UP RIGHT NECK EDGE (80 (80, 80) STS ON NEEDLE). WORK IN K2, P2 RIB FOR 3".

NEXT RND: KNIT INTO FRONT AND BACK OF EVERY ST (160 (160, 160) STS ON NEEDLE).

BO LOOSELY IN KNIT.

CENTER SLEEVES ON SHOULDER SEAMS AND SEW INTO PLACE. SEW SIDE AND SLEEVE SEAMS. WEAVE IN ENDS. BLOCK TO FINISHED MEASUREMENTS. **OPTIONAL:** SEW 2 BUTTONS ABOVE INVERTED "V" ON FRONT BOTTOM.

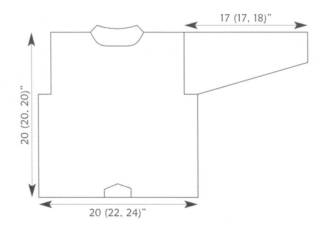

17 (17, 18)"

20 (20, 20)"

20 (22, 24)"

up, down & all around

MATERIALS
YARN: LANA GROSSA "DUE CHINE" - 8 (8, 9) SKEINS COLOR A (#405); 9 (9, 10) SKEINS COLOR B (#406); AND 3 SKEINS LANA GROSSA "BINGO" (#45).
NEEDLES: 32" CIRCULAR US 10½ (7 MM), *OR CORRECT NEEDLE TO OBTAIN GAUGE.*
ACCESSORIES: STITCH HOLDERS.

MEASUREMENTS
CHEST: 44 (48, 52)".
LENGTH: 22 (22, 24)".
SLEEVE LENGTH: 13 (14½, 16½)".

GAUGE
ON US 10½ IN GARTER ST: 12 STS AND 24 ROWS = 4".

NOTES
THE BODY OF THIS SWEATER IS KNITTED FROM SIDE TO SIDE. KEEP EDGES NEAT—ONE FORMS THE BOTTOM HEM AND THERE IS NO HEM FINISHING GIVEN IN THIS PATTERN; HOWEVER, YOU MAY FINISH THE HEM IN ANY WAY YOU LIKE. "GARTER RIDGE" MEANS 2 ROWS.

BACK
WITH US 10½ AND COLOR B, CO 62 (62, 68) STS. WORK IN GARTER ST FOR 3 (3, 3) GARTER RIDGES. CONTINUING THROUGHOUT IN GARTER ST, ([WORK 5 (6, 7) GARTER RIDGES IN COLOR A; 5 (6, 7) GARTER RIDGES IN COLOR B] 5 TIMES); 5 (6, 7) GARTER RIDGES IN COLOR A, AND 3 (3, 3) GARTER RIDGES IN COLOR B. BO.

RIGHT FRONT
WITH US 10½ AND COLOR B, CO 62 (62, 68) STS. WORK IN GARTER ST FOR 3 (3, 3) GARTER RIDGES. CONTINUING THROUGHOUT IN GARTER ST, ([WORK 5 (6, 7) GARTER RIDGES IN COLOR A; WORK 5 (6, 7) GARTER RIDGES IN COLOR B] TWICE).

SHAPE NECK
WORK 5 (6, 7) GARTER RIDGES IN COLOR A, **AND AT SAME TIME,** K2TOG AT END OF 1ST ROW (THIS IS THE NECK EDGE), AND AT NECK EDGE ON EVERY FOLLOWING ROW. WORK 3 (3, 3) GARTER RIDGES IN COLOR B, CONTINUING TO DEC AT NECK EDGE ON EVERY ROW. PLACE REM 46 (44, 48) STS ON HOLDER.

LEFT FRONT
WITH US 10½ AND COLOR B, CO 62 (62, 68) STS. WORK IN GARTER ST FOR 3 (3, 3) GARTER RIDGES. CONTINUING THROUGHOUT IN GARTER ST, ([WORK 5 (6, 7) GARTER RIDGES IN COLOR A; WORK 5 (6, 7) GARTER RIDGES IN COLOR B] TWICE).

SHAPE NECK

WORK 5 (6, 7) GARTER RIDGES IN COLOR A, **AND AT SAME TIME**, K2TOG AT BEG OF 1ST ROW (THIS IS THE NECK EDGE), AND AT NECK EDGE ON EVERY FOLLOWING ROW. WORK 3 (3, 3) GARTER RIDGES IN COLOR B, CONTINUING TO DEC AT NECK EDGE ON EVERY ROW. PLACE REM 46 (44, 48) STS ON HOLDER.

SLEEVES (WORKED FROM SHOULDER TO WRIST)

WITH US 10½ AND COLOR B, CO 52 (52, 56) STS. WORK IN GARTER ST FOR 4 (3, 2) GARTER RIDGES. CONTINUING IN GARTER ST, ([WORK 5 (6, 7) GARTER RIDGES IN COLOR A; WORK 5 (6, 7) GARTER RIDGES IN COLOR B] 3 TIMES); WORK 4 (3, 2) GARTER RIDGES IN COLOR B; **AND AT SAME TIME**, DEC 1 ST AT BEG AND END OF RS ROW OF 4TH (5TH, 5TH) GARTER RIDGE UNTIL 36 (36, 40) STS REM AND STRIPE SEQUENCE GIVEN ABOVE IS COMPLETE.

CUFF

CARRYING 2 STRANDS OF COLOR C TOG, WORK IN ST ST FOR 14 (12, 12) ROWS. BO. EDGES WILL ROLL OUTWARD NATURALLY.

FINISHING

JOIN SHOULDERS AND JOIN SLEEVES TO BODY

WITH US 10½ AND COLOR A, RS'S FACING, PICK UP 1 ST IN EVERY GARTER RIDGE ALONG BACK SHOULDER TO NECK EDGE. WITH ANOTHER US 10½, PICK UP 1 ST IN EVERY GARTER RIDGE ALONG FRONT SHOULDER TO NECK EDGE. JOIN USING 3-NEEDLE BIND-OFF METHOD. USE SAME METHOD TO JOIN SLEEVES TO BODY.

NECK AND FRONT BAND

WITH US 10½, CARRYING 2 STRANDS OF COLOR C TOG, RS FACING, BEG AT BOTTOM RIGHT FRONT EDGE, PICK UP 44 (44, 48) STS UP TO BEG OF NECK SHAPING, 1 (1, 1) ST TO CLOSE CORNER, 18 (18, 20) STS UP RIGHT NECK EDGE, 16 (18, 20) STS ALONG BACK NECK EDGE, 18 (18, 20) STS DOWN LEFT NECK EDGE, 1 (1, 1) ST TO CLOSE CORNER, AND 44 (44, 48) STS DOWN LEFT FRONT EDGE (142 (142, 158) STS ON NEEDLE). WORK BACK AND FORTH IN ST ST FOR 12 ROWS. BO. SEW FRONT TOG FROM BOTTOM EDGE UP TO NECK SHAPING IN APPROX. 4TH ROW FROM PICKED-UP EDGE. THE FRONT EDGES WILL ROLL OUTWARD NATURALLY.

SEW ROLLED EDGE TO BACK OF NECK, IF DESIRED. SEW SIDE AND SLEEVE SEAMS. WEAVE IN ENDS. BLOCK TO FINISHED MEASUREMENTS.

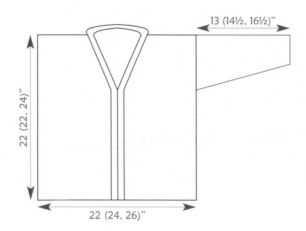

ruffles & flourishes

MATERIALS

YARN: Lana Grossa "Bingo" - 3 (3, 4) skeins Color A (#51); 3 (3, 4) skeins Color B (#44); 2 (2, 2) skeins Color C (#24); 3 (4, 4) skeins Color D (#7); 4 (4, 6) skeins Color E (#73); and 1 (2, 2) skein(s) Color F (#62).
NEEDLES: US 7 (4.5 mm), *OR CORRECT NEEDLE TO OBTAIN GAUGE.*

MEASUREMENTS

CHEST: 44 (46, 48)".
LENGTH: 22 (23, 24)".
SLEEVE LENGTH: 22 (22, 22)".

GAUGE

On US 7 in st st: 18 sts and 23 rows = 4".

BACK

With US 7 and Color A (D, E), CO 196 (208, 220) sts. Following **STRIPE SEQUENCE FOR BACK AND FRONT** (PAGE 20) throughout, work as follows:

ROW 1 (WS): Purl.
ROW 2 (RS): ([K2TOG] to end) (98 (104, 110) sts rem).

ROW 3 (WS): K1, *k3, p3**; rep from * to **; end p1.

Rep Row 3 until piece measures 5 (5, 5)" from CO edge.

CHANGE TO ST ST AND CONTINUE STRIPE SEQUENCE UNTIL PIECE MEASURES 11½ (12½, 13½)" FROM CO EDGE, ENDING WITH RS FACING FOR NEXT ROW.

SHAPE ARMHOLES
BO 4 STS AT BEG OF NEXT 2 ROWS.

NEXT ROW (RS): K2, SSK; KNIT TO LAST 4 STS; K2TOG, K2.
NEXT ROW (WS): PURL.

REP LAST 2 ROWS UNTIL 76 (80, 84) STS REM. CONTINUE WITHOUT FURTHER SHAPING UNTIL ARMHOLE MEASURES 9½ (9½, 9½)", ENDING WITH RS FACING FOR NEXT ROW.

SHAPE SHOULDERS AND BACK NECK
NEXT ROW (RS): BO 7 (8, 8) STS; K15 (15, 17) AND PLACE THESE STS ON HOLDER FOR RIGHT SHOULDER; BO NEXT 32 (34, 34) STS FOR BACK NECK; KNIT TO END.

NEXT ROW (WS): BO 7 (8, 8) STS; PURL TO END.
NEXT ROW (RS): KNIT.
NEXT ROW (WS): BO 7 (8, 8) STS; PURL TO END.
NEXT ROW (RS): BO 3 (3, 3) STS; KNIT TO END.
NEXT ROW (WS): BO REM 5 (4, 6) STS.

WITH RS FACING, PLACE STS FROM HOLDER ONTO LEFT-HAND NEEDLE, REJOIN YARN, AND WORK RIGHT SHOULDER AS FOR LEFT SHOULDER, REVERSING SHAPING.

FRONT
WORK AS FOR BACK UNTIL PIECE MEASURES 18 (19, 20)" FROM CO EDGE, ENDING WITH RS FACING FOR NEXT ROW.

SHAPE FRONT NECK
NEXT ROW (RS): K30 (31, 33); BO NEXT 16 (18, 18) STS; K30 (31, 33).
NEXT ROW (WS): PURL.

WORKING EACH SIDE SEPARATELY, BO 2 STS AT NECK EDGE ON NEXT ROW, THEN EVERY FOLLOWING RS ROW 2 (2, 2) TIMES, THEN EVERY FOLLOWING 4TH ROW ONCE (21 (23, 25) STS REM), ENDING WITH RS FACING FOR NEXT ROW.

SHAPE SHOULDER
NEXT ROW (RS): BO 7 (8, 8) STS; KNIT TO END.
NEXT ROW (WS): PURL.
NEXT ROW (RS): BO 7 (8, 8) STS; KNIT TO END.

NEXT ROW (WS): PURL.
NEXT ROW (RS): BO REM 8 (7, 9) STS.

SLEEVES
WITH US 7 AND COLOR E (E, E) CO 100 (100, 100) STS. FOLLOWING **STRIPE SEQUENCE FOR SLEEVES** (PAGE 20) THROUGHOUT, WORK AS FOLLOWS:

ROW 1 (WS): PURL.
ROW 2 (RS): ([K2TOG] TO END) (50 (50, 50) STS REM).

ROW 3 (WS): K1, *K3, P3**; REP FROM * TO **; END P1.

REP ROW 3 UNTIL PIECE MEASURES 3½ (3½, 3½)" FROM CO EDGE.

CHANGE TO ST ST AND CONTINUE STRIPE SEQUENCE, **AND AT SAME TIME,** INC 1 ST AT BEG AND END OF NEXT AND EVERY FOLLOWING 10TH (10TH, 10TH) ROW AS FOLLOWS: K2, M1, KNIT TO LAST 2 STS, M1, K2, UNTIL THERE ARE 60 (62, 64) STS, THEN EVERY FOLLOWING 4TH ROW UNTIL THERE ARE 68 (70, 72) STS. CONTINUE WITHOUT FURTHER SHAPING UNTIL STRIPE SEQUENCE IS AT SAME POINT AS BODY ARMHOLE SHAPING, ENDING WITH RS FACING FOR NEXT ROW.

SHAPE SLEEVE TOP
BO 4 STS AT BEG OF NEXT 2 ROWS (60 (62, 64) STS REM). DEC 1 ST AT BEG AND END OF NEXT AND EVERY FOLLOWING 4TH ROW UNTIL 54 (56, 58) STS REM. WORK 1 ROW, THEN DEC 1 ST AT BEG AND END OF EVERY ALT ROW 11 TIMES (32 (34, 36) STS REM), THEN DEC 3 STS EVERY ROW 6 TIMES. BO REM 14 (16, 18) STS.

JOIN SHOULDERS
SEW BACK AND FRONT SHOULDERS TOG.

NECK
WITH US 7 AND COLOR C (C, C), RS FACING, BEG AT LEFT SHOULDER SEAM PICK UP 14 (16, 16) STS DOWN LEFT NECK EDGE, 17 (18, 18) STS ALONG FRONT NECK EDGE, 14 (16, 16) STS UP RIGHT NECK EDGE AND 39 (40, 40) STS ALONG BACK NECK EDGE (84 (90, 90) STS ON NEEDLE). FOLLOWING **STRIPE SEQUENCE FOR NECK** (PAGE 20), JOIN, AND WORK IN K3, P3 RIB FOR 3½ (3½, 3½)". BO WITH COLOR B (B, B).

Finishing

Center sleeves on shoulder seams and sew into place. Sew side and sleeve seams. Weave in ends. Block to finished measurements.

Stripe Sequence for Back and Front

Beg 3rd Size	2 rows Color F	2 rows Color F
7 rows Color E	3 rows Color D	8 rows Color D
2 Rows Color F	9 rows Color B	6 rows Color A
Beg 2nd Size	1 row Color A	4 rows Color B
6 rows Color D	4 rows Color C	2 rows Color E
1 row Color B	1 row Color A	1 row Color C
Beg 1st Size	3 rows Color E	2 rows Color E
5 rows Color A	2 rows Color F	1 row Color C
2 rows Color B	6 rows Color D	2 rows Color E
3 rows Color C	1 row Color C	1 row Color C
8 rows Color D	7 rows Color A	2 rows Color E
4 rows Color E	5 rows Color B	2 rows Color F
2 rows Color B	2 rows Color E	2 rows Color A
2 rows Color F	2 rows Color B	3 rows Color D
1 row Color C	4 rows Color E	End All Sizes
4 rows Color A	2 rows Color F	
6 rows Color E	2 rows Color C	

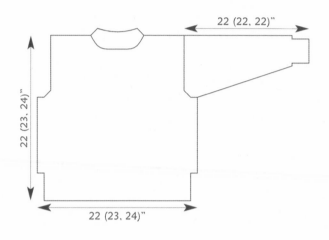

Stripe Sequence for Sleeves

Beg All Sizes	4 rows Color A	5 rows Color B
7 rows Color E	6 rows Color E	2 rows Color E
2 rows Color F	2 rows Color F	2 rows Color B
6 rows Color D	3 rows Color D	4 rows Color E
2 rows Color B	9 rows Color B	2 rows Color F
6 rows Color A	1 row Color A	2 rows Color C
2 rows Color B	4 rows Color C	2 rows Color F
3 rows Color C	1 row Color A	8 rows Color D
8 rows Color D	3 rows Color E	6 rows Color A
4 rows Color E	2 rows Color F	4 rows Color B
2 rows Color B	6 rows Color D	4 rows Color E
2 rows Color F	1 row Color C	End All Sizes
1 row Color C	7 rows Color A	

Stripe Sequence for Neck

Beg All Sizes	2 rows Color F	2 rows Color C
1 row Color C	4 rows Color D	6 rows Color A
5 rows Color B	4 rows Color E	End All Sizes

prato

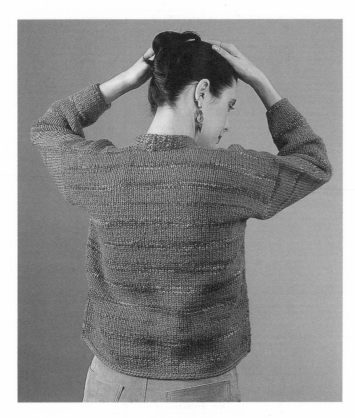

MATERIALS

YARN: LANA GROSSA "INSERTO" - 14 (15, 16, 17) SKEINS.
GARMENT SHOWN IN #5.
NEEDLES: US 9 (5.5 MM), *OR CORRECT NEEDLE TO OBTAIN GAUGE.* SIZE H CROCHET HOOK.
ACCESSORIES: STITCH HOLDERS.

MEASUREMENTS

CHEST: 40 (44, 48, 52)".
LENGTH: 21 (22, 23, 24)".
SLEEVE LENGTH: 16 (16½, 17, 17½)".

GAUGE

ON US 9 IN ST ST: 14 STS AND 21 ROWS = 4".

BACK

WITH US 9, CO 70 (77, 84, 91) STS. WORK IN ST ST UNTIL PIECE MEASURES 21 (22, 23, 24)" FROM CO EDGE. ON LAST ROW, WORK 24 (27, 30, 33) STS AND PLACE ON HOLDER FOR RIGHT SHOULDER; BO NEXT 22 (23, 24, 25) STS, WORK 24 (27, 30, 33) STS AND PLACE ON ANOTHER HOLDER FOR LEFT SHOULDER.

RIGHT FRONT

WITH US 9, CO 42 (45, 48, 51) STS. WORK IN ST ST UNTIL PIECE MEASURES 15 (16, 17, 18)" FROM CO EDGE, ENDING WITH RS FACING FOR NEXT ROW.

SHAPE NECK

NEXT ROW (RS): K10 (10, 10, 10), SSK, K30 (33, 36, 39).
NEXT ROW (WS): PURL.
NEXT ROW (RS): K10 (10, 10, 10), SSK, K29 (32, 35, 38).
NEXT ROW (WS): PURL.
NEXT ROW (RS): K10 (10, 10, 10), SSK, K28 (31, 34, 37).
NEXT ROW (WS): PURL.
NEXT ROW (RS): K10 (10, 10, 10), SSK, K27 (30, 33, 36).
NEXT ROW (WS): PURL.
NEXT ROW (RS): K10 (10, 10, 10), SSK, K26 (29, 32, 35).
NEXT ROW (WS): PURL.
NEXT ROW (RS): K10 (10, 10, 10), SSK, K25 (28, 31, 34).
NEXT ROW (WS): PURL.
NEXT ROW (RS): K10 (10, 10, 10), SSK, K24 (27, 30, 33).
NEXT ROW (WS): PURL.
NEXT ROW (RS): K10 (10, 10, 10), SSK, K23 (26, 29, 32).

CONTINUE WITHOUT FURTHER SHAPING UNTIL PIECE MEASURES 21 (22, 23, 24)" FROM CO EDGE. PLACE FIRST

10 (10, 10, 10) STS ON HOLDER FOR NECK AND NEXT 24 (27, 30, 33) STS ON ANOTHER HOLDER FOR RIGHT SHOULDER.

LEFT FRONT

WITH US 9, CO 42 (45, 48, 51) STS. WORK IN ST ST UNTIL PIECE MEASURES 15 (16, 17, 18)" FROM CO EDGE, ENDING WITH RS FACING FOR NEXT ROW.

SHAPE NECK

NEXT ROW (RS): K30 (33, 36, 39), K2TOG, K10 (10, 10, 10).
NEXT ROW (WS): PURL.
NEXT ROW (RS): K29 (32, 35, 38), K2TOG, K10 (10, 10, 10).
NEXT ROW (WS): PURL.
NEXT ROW (RS): K28 (31, 34, 37), K2TOG, K10 (10, 10, 10).
NEXT ROW (WS): PURL.
NEXT ROW (RS): K27 (30, 33, 36), K2TOG, K10 (10, 10, 10).
NEXT ROW (WS): PURL.
NEXT ROW (RS): K26 (29, 32, 35), K2TOG, K10 (10, 10, 10).
NEXT ROW (WS): PURL.
NEXT ROW (RS): K25 (28, 31, 34); K2TOG, K10 (10, 10, 10).
NEXT ROW (WS): PURL.
NEXT ROW (RS): K24 (27, 30, 33), K2TOG, K10 (10, 10, 10).
NEXT ROW (WS): PURL.
NEXT ROW (RS): K23 (26, 29, 32), K2TOG, K10 (10, 10, 10).

CONTINUE WITHOUT FURTHER SHAPING UNTIL PIECE MEASURES 21 (22, 23, 24)" FROM CO EDGE. PLACE FIRST 10 (10, 10, 10) STS ON HOLDER FOR NECK AND LAST 24 (27, 30, 33) STS ON ANOTHER HOLDER FOR LEFT SHOULDER.

JOIN SHOULDERS

WITH RS'S FACING, JOIN SHOULDERS USING 3-NEEDLE BIND-OFF METHOD.

COLLAR

WITH US 9, WORK 10 (10, 10, 10) STS FROM HOLDER FOR RIGHT NECK UNTIL PIECE WILL FIT FROM SHOULDER SEAM TO CENTER BACK NECK. WITH ANOTHER US 9, WORK 10 (10, 10, 10) STS FROM HOLDER FOR LEFT NECK UNTIL PIECE WILL FIT FROM SHOULDER SEAM TO CENTER BACK NECK. GRAFT OR USE 3-NEEDLE BIND-OFF METHOD TO JOIN RIGHT AND LEFT NECK TOG AT CENTER BACK NECK. SEW TO BACK OF NECK.

SLEEVES

WITH US 9, CO 42 (44, 46, 50) STS. WORK IN ST ST, **AND AT SAME TIME**, INC 1 ST AT BEG AND END OF EVERY 6TH ROW 12 (13, 14, 15) TIMES (66 (70, 74, 80) STS ON NEEDLE). WORK WITHOUT FURTHER SHAPING UNTIL PIECE MEASURES 16 (16½, 17, 17½)" FROM CO EDGE. BO.

FINISHING

CENTER SLEEVES ON SHOULDER SEAMS AND SEW INTO PLACE. SEW SIDE AND SLEEVE SEAMS. WITH H CROCHET HOOK, RS FACING, LOOSELY CROCHET 1 ROW OF SINGLE CROCHET ALONG BOTTOM EDGE. REP FOR CUFFS. THE FRONT EDGES AND COLLAR WILL ROLL INWARD NATURALLY.

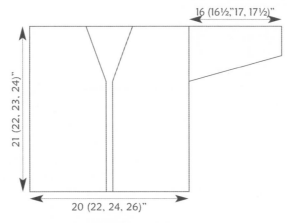

16 (16½," 17, 17½)"

21 (22, 23, 24)"

20 (22, 24, 26)"

toscana

Materials

Yarn: Lana Grossa "Due Chine" - 7 (8, 8) skeins Color A (#404); 5 (5, 6) skeins Color B (#408); 4 (4, 4) skeins Color C (#402); 2 (2, 2) skeins Color D, (#401); 2 (2, 2) skeins Color E (#405); 4 (4, 5) skeins Color F (#406); and 1 (1, 1) skein Color G (#407).

Needles: US 13 (9 mm), *or correct needle to obtain gauge.* 2 short double-pointed US 7 (4.5 mm).

Measurements

Chest: 42 (46, 50)".
Length: 26 (26, 27)".
Sleeve Length: 18 (18, 18½)".

Gauge

On US 13 in Woven Stitch: 16 sts and 23 rows = 4".

Woven Stitch (over even no. of sts)

Row 1 (RS): *K1, yf, sl1 purlwise, yb**; rep from * to **.

Row 2 (WS): *P1, yb, sl1 purlwise, yf**; rep from * to **.

Rep Rows 1 and 2.

Double Increases

Row 1 (RS): K1, yf, sl1 purlwise, yb; knit into front and back of next st; work in pattern to last 2 sts; knit into front and back of next st; yf sl1.

Row 2 (WS): P1, yb, sl1 purlwise; pick up loop of next st 1 row below and purl into back of this st; yb, sl1 purlwise; work in pattern to last 3 sts; pick up loop of next st 1 row below and purl into back of this st; yb, sl1 purlwise, k1, yb, sl1.

Applied Corded Edging

With short double-pointed US 7 and Color C, CO 3 sts. With same needle, WS facing, *pick up 1 st; slide all 4 sts to opposite end of needle; k2, k2tog**; rep from * to **.

Back

With US 13 and Color A, CO 96 (102, 112) sts. With WS facing, work Row 2 of Woven Stitch, then rep Rows 1 and 2 of Woven Stitch, following Stripe Sequence for Back and Fronts (page 26); AND AT SAME TIME, when back measures 5" and with RS facing, BO 6 sts at beg of next 2 rows (84 (90, 100) sts rem). Continue without further shaping until you have completed Row 142 (142, 148), ending with WS facing.

Next Row (Last Row of Color A Stripe) (WS): Work 30 (32, 36) sts, BO next 24 (26, 28) sts, work to end of row.

Working each side separately, work 4 more rows. Place shoulder sts on holders.

Left Front

With US 13 and Color A, CO 38 (42, 46) sts. With WS facing, work 1 row in Woven Stitch. Work Double Increases on next 2 rows, then work 2 rows without incs. Rep these 4 rows once more (46 (50, 54) sts on needle). Following Stripe Sequence for Back and Fronts, work until piece measures 11½ (11½, 11½)" from CO edge, ending with RS facing for next row.

Shape Lapel

On next 2 rows, at front edge only, work Double Increases (one on each row). Rep these paired incs every 11th & 12th row 4 times (56 (60, 64) sts on needle). On Row 126 (126, 133) (Row 8 of Color F), shape neck:

Shape Neck

At front edge, BO 10 (11, 12) sts once, 3 (3, 3) sts once, 2 (2, 2) sts twice, then 1 (1, 1) st at neck edge on every row 9 (10, 9) times. Work to end of Stripe Sequence for Back and Fronts, ending with RS facing for next row. Place sts on holder.

Right Front

Work same as for Left Front, reversing all shaping; AND AT SAME TIME, when piece measures 6 (6, 6)" from cast-on edge, Make Buttonhole as follows: With RS facing, work 3 sts in Woven Stitch, yf, sl1 knitwise, yb; *sl1 from left-hand needle to right-hand needle; pass 1st sl st over**; rep from * to ** twice more (3 sts bound off). Turn work; CO 4 sts using cable cast-on method, and moving yarn to front between 3rd & 4th cast-on sts. Turn work. Sl1 from left-hand needle to right-hand needle and pass last cast-on st over this st. Work to end.

When piece measures 11½ (11½, 11½)" from cast-on edge, Make Buttonhole as above.

Sleeves

With US 13 and Color A, CO 44 (48, 52) sts. Beg with WS facing, work in Woven Stitch, following Stripe Sequence for Sleeves (page 26), AND AT SAME TIME, work Double Increases on Rows 6 and 7, then every 11th and 12th rows, until there are 76 (80, 84) sts on needle, working to end of color stripe sequence (sleeve will measure 18 (18, 18½)" from CO edge). BO tightly.

COLLAR

With US 13 and Color A, CO 40 (40, 42) sts. Beg with WS facing, work in **Woven Stitch** as follows: Work 1 row. CO 3 (4, 4) sts at beg of next 8 rows. Work 2 rows, then work **Double Increases** on next 2 rows. Rep these last 4 rows once more (72 (80, 82) sts on needle). Work without further shaping until collar measures approx. 4 (4½, 4¼)". BO tightly. Work 1 row of **Applied Corded Edging** around edge of collar.

POCKETS (MAKE 2)

With US 13 and Color A, CO 22 sts. Beg with WS facing, work 1 row in **Woven Stitch**. Work **Double Increases** on next 2 rows. Continue in **Woven Stitch** following **Stripe Sequence for Pockets**. BO tightly.

Work 1 row of **Applied Corded Edging** along top edge of pocket.

FINISHING

Block pieces to finished measurements. Join shoulders using 3-needle bind-off method. Sew sleeve seams. Sew side seams, leaving 5" unsewn at bottom for side vents. Sew right side of collar to wrong side of neck. Whipstitch back side vent extensions to WS of left and right fronts. Work 1 row of **Applied Corded Edging** beg at top of right front lapel, continuing down right front, along bottom of right front, around side vent, along bottom of back, around side vent, along bottom of left front, and up left front, ending at top of left front lapel. Work **Applied Corded Edging** on sleeve cuffs, beg and ending at seam. Sew on buttons opposite buttonholes. Sew pockets to right front and left front, matching stripes. Weave in ends.

STRIPE SEQUENCE FOR BACK AND FRONTS

23 (23, 27) rows Color A	6 (6, 6) rows Color G
10 (10, 12) rows Color B	16 (16, 16) rows Color B
	4 (4, 4) rows Color F
2 (2, 2) rows Color C	
2 (2, 2) rows Color D	2 (2, 2) rows Color C
2 (2, 2) rows Color C	2 (2, 2) rows Color D
	2 (2, 2) rows Color C
5 (5, 5) rows Color E	
18 (18, 18) rows Color F	6 (6, 6) rows Color E
12 (12, 12) rows Color A	9 (9, 9) rows Color F
	16 (16, 16) rows Color A
2 (2, 2) rows Color C	
2 (2, 2) rows Color D	2 (2, 2) rows Color C
2 (2, 2) rows Color C	2 (2, 2) rows Color D
	2 (2, 2) rows Color C

STRIPE SEQUENCE FOR POCKETS

15 (15, 17) rows Color A
10 (10, 12) rows Color B

2 (2, 2) rows Color C
2 (2, 2) rows Color D
2 (2, 2) rows Color C

STRIPE SEQUENCE FOR SLEEVES

14 (14, 18) rows Color A	2 rows Color C
10 (10, 12) rows Color B	2 rows Color D
	2 rows Color C
2 (2, 2) rows Color C	
2 (2, 2) rows Color D	6 rows Color G
2 (2, 2) rows Color C	16 rows Color B
	4 rows Color F
5 rows Color E	
18 rows Color F	2 rows Color C
12 rows Color A	2 rows Color D
	2 rows Color C

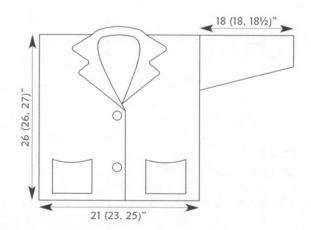

18 (18, 18½)"
26 (26, 27)"
21 (23, 25)"

grey flannel jazz

MATERIALS

YARN: LANA GROSSA "MERINO BIG" - 6 (6, 7) SKEINS EACH OF COLOR A (#618) AND COLOR B (#617); 1 (1, 1) SKEIN EACH OF COLOR C (#608), COLOR D (#632), COLOR E (#649) AND COLOR F (#625).
NEEDLES: 24" CIRCULAR US 5 (3.75 MM); 24" AND 40" CIRCULAR US 6 (4 MM), *OR CORRECT NEEDLES TO OBTAIN GAUGE.*
ACCESSORIES: STITCH HOLDERS.

MEASUREMENTS

CHEST: 44 (48, 52)".
LENGTH: 22 (22, 23)".
SLEEVE LENGTH: 16 (16, 17)".

GAUGE

ON US 6 IN ST ST: 20 STS AND 28 ROWS = 4".

BACK

WITH US 5 AND COLOR A, CO 110 (120, 130) STS. WORK IN k1, p1 RIB FOR 5 ROWS. CHANGE TO US 6 AND WORK IN ST ST FOR ANOTHER 23 (23, 25) ROWS (THERE WILL BE 28 (28, 30) TOTAL ROWS IN COLOR A). CONTINUING THROUGHOUT IN ST ST, ([WORK 28 (28, 30) ROWS IN COLOR B; WORK 28 (28, 30) ROWS IN COLOR A] TWICE), THEN WORK 14 (14, 15) ROWS IN COLOR B. ON LAST ROW, WORK 36 (41, 46) STS AND PLACE ON HOLDER FOR RIGHT SHOULDER, BO 38 (38, 38) STS FOR BACK NECK, WORK 36 (41, 46) STS AND PLACE ON HOLDER FOR LEFT SHOULDER.

LEFT FRONT

WITH US 5 AND COLOR A, CO 55 (60, 65) STS. WORK IN k1, p1 RIB FOR 5 ROWS. CHANGE TO US 6 AND WORK IN ST ST FOR ANOTHER 23 (23, 25) ROWS (THERE WILL BE 28 (28, 30) TOTAL ROWS IN COLOR A). CONTINUING THROUGHOUT IN ST ST, WORK 28 (28, 30) ROWS IN

COLOR B; WORK 28 (28, 30) ROWS IN COLOR A. CHANGE TO COLOR B.

SHAPE NECK
NEXT ROW (RS) (DEC ROW): KNIT TO LAST 3 STS; K2TOG, K1.

CONTINUING IN STRIPE SEQUENCE AS SET, WORK **DEC ROW** EVERY 4TH ROW 16 MORE TIMES, THEN EVERY 2ND ROW TWICE. WORK ON REM 36 (41, 46) STS UNTIL SAME LENGTH AS BACK. PLACE SHOULDER STS ON HOLDER.

RIGHT FRONT
WORK SAME AS FOR LEFT FRONT, WORKING **DEC ROW** AS FOLLOWS:

(RS) (DEC ROW): K1, K2TOG; KNIT TO END OF ROW.

JOIN SHOULDERS
WITH RS'S FACING, JOIN SHOULDERS USING 3-NEEDLE BIND-OFF METHOD.

SLEEVES (WORKED FROM SHOULDER TO WRIST)
WITH US 6 AND COLOR B, CO 94 (94, 100) STS. WORK IN ST ST FOR 28 (28, 30) ROWS, THEN CONTINUING THROUGHOUT IN ST ST, WORK 28 (28, 30) ROWS IN COLOR A, 28 (28, 30) ROWS IN COLOR B, AND 28 (28, 30) ROWS IN COLOR A, **AND AT SAME TIME**, DEC 1 ST AT BEG AND END OF EVERY 4TH ROW 4 TIMES, THEN EVERY 6TH ROW 15 TIMES (56 (56, 62) STS REM AND SLEEVE MEASURES APPROX. 16 (17, 17)"). CONTINUING IN ST ST, WORK 4 ROWS IN COLOR C, 4 ROWS IN COLOR D, 4 ROWS IN COLOR E, AND 2 ROWS IN COLOR F.

NEXT ROW (RS) (PICOT EDGE): WITH COLOR F, K2, *YO, K2TOG**; REP FROM * TO **; END K2.
NEXT ROW (WS): PURL.

CONTINUING IN ST ST, WORK 2 MORE ROWS IN COLOR F, 4 ROWS IN COLOR E, 4 ROWS IN COLOR D, 10 ROWS IN COLOR C AND 10 ROWS IN COLOR B. BO.

FINISHING
PLACE MARKERS APPROX. 9½ (9½, 10)" DOWN FROM SHOULDER SEAM ON BOTH FRONT AND BACK AND SEW SLEEVES TO BODY BETWEEN MARKERS. SEW SIDE AND SLEEVE SEAMS. FOLD SLEEVE CUFF ON PICOT EDGE AND SEW TO INSIDE. FOLD CUFF BACK AND TACK TO SLEEVE SEAM.

FRONT BORDER
WITH 40" US 6 CIRCULAR AND COLOR C, RS FACING, PICK UP 102 (102, 108) STS UP RIGHT FRONT EDGE, 37 (37, 37) STS ACROSS BACK NECK, AND 102 (102, 108) STS DOWN LEFT FRONT EDGE (241 (241, 253) STS ON NEEDLE). TURN, AND WORK IN ST ST AS FOLLOWS:

NEXT ROW (WS): PURL, DEC'G 3 STS EVENLY ALONG BACK NECK.

CONTINUING IN ST ST, WORK 2 MORE ROWS IN COLOR C, 4 ROWS IN COLOR D, 4 ROWS IN COLOR E AND 2 ROWS IN COLOR F.

NEXT ROW (RS) (PICOT EDGE): WITH COLOR F, K2, *YO, K2TOG**; REP FROM * TO **; END K2.

NEXT ROW (WS): PURL.

CONTINUING IN ST ST, WORK 2 MORE ROWS IN COLOR F, 4 ROWS IN COLOR E, 4 ROWS IN COLOR D AND 3 ROWS IN COLOR C. BO.

FOLD BORDER TO INSIDE ALONG PICOT EDGE AND TACK TO INSIDE. WEAVE IN ENDS. BLOCK TO FINISHED MEASUREMENTS.

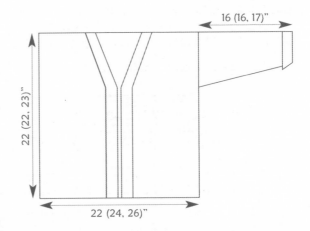

16 (16, 17)"

22 (22, 23)"

22 (24, 26)"

waiting for godet

MATERIALS

YARN: Lana Grossa "Bingo" or "Bingo Chine" - 15 (16, 17) skeins. Garment shown in "Bingo" Color #75 and "Bingo Chine" Color #507.
NEEDLES: US 7 (4.5 mm), *OR CORRECT NEEDLE TO OBTAIN GAUGE.*
ACCESSORIES: Stitch holders. Five 5/8" buttons.

MEASUREMENTS

CHEST: 37 (42, 49)".
LENGTH: 21 (22, 23)".
SLEEVE LENGTH: 18 (18½, 18½)".

GAUGE

On US 7 in st st: 16 sts and 24 rows = 4".

ABOUT CHARTS

Read odd-numbered (RS) rows (1-17) from right to left and even-numbered (WS) rows (0-18) from left to right.

BACK

With US 8, CO 192 (192, 200) sts. Work in garter st for 22 rows, ending with WS facing for next row. Beg and ending at points marked for your size, work Chart A. When Chart A is complete, there will be 90 (90, 98) sts on needle.

1ST SIZE ONLY: Continue in st st, dec'g 1 st at beg and end of next row, then every 4th row 3 more times (82 sts rem).

ALL SIZES: Continue in st st on rem 82 (90, 98) sts until piece measures 10 (10½, 11½)" from CO edge, ending with RS facing for next row.

SHAPE ARMHOLE

BO 4 sts at beg of next 2 rows. Continue in st st on rem 74 (82, 90) sts until piece measures 20½ (21½, 22½)" from CO edge, ending with RS facing for next row.

SHAPE BACK NECK

NEXT ROW (RS): K25 (29, 30) sts, BO next 24 (24, 30) sts, k25 (29, 30) sts.

Working each side separately, turn, and purl next row. Place shoulder sts on separate holders.

LEFT FRONT

With US 8, CO 99 (99, 103) sts. Work in garter st for 22 rows, ending with WS facing for next row. Beg and ending at points marked for your size, work Chart B. When Chart B is complete, there will be 48 (48, 52) sts on needle.

1ST SIZE ONLY: Continuing in st st (working buttonband in garter st as set), dec 1 st at beg of next row, then every 4th row 2 more times (45 sts rem).

ALL SIZES: Continue as set on rem 45 (48, 52) sts until piece measures 10 (10½, 11½)" from CO edge, ending with RS facing for next row.

SHAPE ARMHOLE
BO 4 sts at beg of next row. Continue as set on rem 41 (44, 48) sts until piece measures 17 (18, 19)" from CO edge, ending with WS facing for next row.

NEXT ROW (WS): BO 5 buttonband sts, knit to end.

SHAPE FRONT NECK
Continuing as set, BO 3 sts at neck edge twice and 2 sts 2 (3, 5) times, then dec 1 (1, 0) st (1, 1, 0) time. Work without further shaping on rem 25 (29, 30) sts until piece measures same as back. Place sts on holder.

RIGHT FRONT
With US 8, CO 99 (99, 103) sts. Work in garter st for 22 rows, ending with WS facing for next row. Beg and ending at points marked for your size, work Chart C. When Chart C is complete, there will be 48 (48, 52) sts on needle.

NEXT ROW (RS) (BUTTONHOLE ROW): K2; move yarn to front of work, sl1 knitwise; move yarn to back; sl next st on left-hand needle knitwise, pass 1st sl st over; return st to left-hand needle; turn work; pick up yarn, CO 2 sts using cable cast-on method; bring yarn to front between 2 cast-on sts; turn work; slip 1st st from left-hand to right-hand needle and pass slipped st over; knit to end of row.

1ST SIZE: Continue in st st (working **Buttonhole Row** every 18 rows), dec'g 1 st at end of every 4th row 3 more times (44 sts rem). **2ND & 3RD SIZE:** Continue in st st (working **Buttonhole Row** every 20 rows).

ALL SIZES: Continue as set on rem 44 (48, 52) sts until piece measures 10 (10½, 11½)" from CO edge, ending with WS facing for next row.

SHAPE ARMHOLE
BO 4 sts at beg of next row. Continue as set on rem 40 (44, 48) sts until piece measures 17 (18, 19)" from CO edge, ending with RS facing for next row.

NEXT ROW (RS): BO 5 buttonband sts, knit to end.

SHAPE FRONT NECK
Continuing as set, BO 3 sts at neck edge once, and 2 sts 3 (3, 5) times, then dec 1 (1, 0) st (1, 1, 0) time. Work without further shaping on rem 25 (29, 30) sts until piece measures same as back. Place sts on holder.

SLEEVES
With US 8, CO 54 (54, 58) sts. Work in garter st for 8 rows, ending with WS facing for next row. Beg and ending at points marked for your size, work Chart A. When Chart A is complete, there will be 37 (37 41) sts on needle. Continue in st st, inc'g 1 st at beg and end of every 3rd row 24 (24, 24) times (85, 85, 89) sts on needle. Work without further shaping until sleeve measures 18 (18½, 18½)" from CO edge. BO.

JOIN SHOULDERS
With RS's facing, join shoulders using 3-needle bind-off method.

COLLAR
With US 8, RS facing, beg at right neck edge (omitting buttonband), pick up 27 (29, 28) sts up right neck edge, 24 (24, 30) sts along back neck edge, and 27 (29, 28) sts down left neck edge (78, 82, 86) sts on needle). Work in garter st for 8 rows, then inc 1 st at beg and end of next row, then every 4th row until collar measures 5 (5, 5)". BO.

FINISHING
Center sleeves on shoulder seams and sew into place. Sew side and sleeve seams. Sew on buttons opposite buttonholes. Weave in ends. Block to finished measurements.

CHART A (BACK RUFFLE & SLEEVE CUFF)

Rep 6 (6, 6) Times for Back
Rep 1 (1, 1) Time for Sleeve

End 3rd Size Sleeve
End 1st & 2nd Size Sleeve
End 3rd Size Back
End 1st & 2nd Size Back
Beg 1st & 2nd Size Back
Beg 3rd Size Back
Beg 1st & 2nd Size Sleeve
Beg 3rd Size Sleeve

Foundation Row

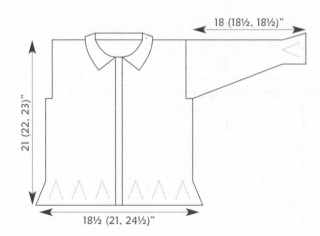

18 (18½, 18½)"

21 (22, 23)"

18½ (21, 24½)"

KEY

I	K ON RIGHT SIDE ROWS ; P ON WRONG SIDE ROWS .
—	P ON RIGHT SIDE ROWS ; K ON WRONG SIDE ROWS .
/	K2TOG.
△	P3TOGTBL.
B	MAKE BOBBLE : ([K1, P1, K1, P1, K1] IN SAME ST); SL 4TH, 3RD, 2ND AND 1ST OVER LAST ST MADE.
■	NO STITCH.

Chart B (Left Front Ruffle)

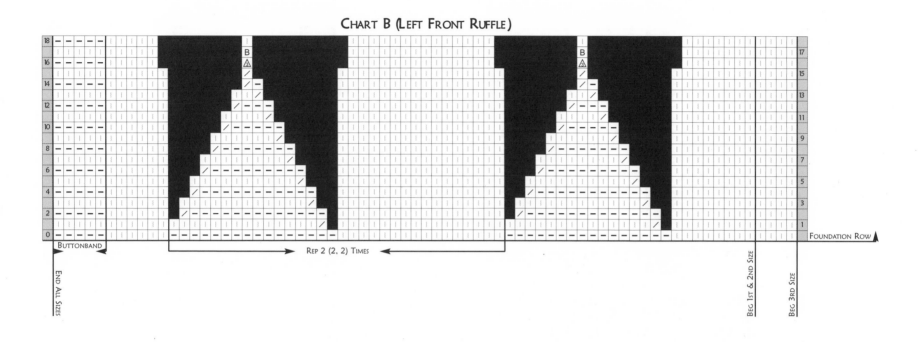

Chart C (Right Front Ruffle)

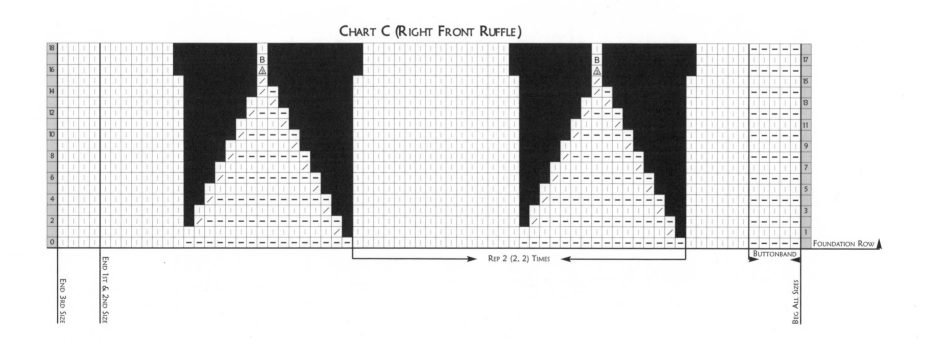

baggy

MATERIALS

YARN: Lana Grossa "Royal Tweed" - 12 (13, 15, 16) skeins. Garment shown in #10.

NEEDLES: 24" US 8 (5 mm) and 16" US 8 (5 mm) and US 9 (5.5 mm), *or correct needles to obtain gauge.*

ACCESSORIES: Stitch holders.

MEASUREMENTS

CHEST: 42 (46, 50, 54)".
LENGTH: 26 (26, 28, 28)".
SLEEVE LENGTH: 17 (17, 18, 18)".

GAUGE

ON US 8 IN **FISHERMAN'S RIB**: 14 STS AND 32 ROWS = 4".

RIBBING
ROW 1 (WS): *K1, P1**; REP FROM * TO **; END K1.
ROW 2 (RS): *P1, K1**; REP FROM * TO **; END P1.

REP ROWS 1 AND 2.

NECK RIBBING
RND 1: *P1, K1**; REP FROM * TO **.

REP RND 1.

FISHERMAN'S RIB
ROW 1 (RS): *K1, K1 IN ROW BELOW**; REP FROM * TO **; END K1.
ROW 2 (WS): K2; *K1 IN ROW BELOW, K1**; REP FROM * TO **; END K1.

REP ROWS 1 AND 2.

DECREASE PATTERN
NOTE: WHEN WORKING SSK OR K2TOG, WORK KNIT STS INTO ROW BELOW TO MAINTAIN PROMINENCE OF RIB AT DEC LINE.

ROW 1 (RS): K5, SSK; WORK IN PATTERN TO LAST 7 STS; K2TOG, K5.
ROW 2 & 4 (WS): K6; WORK IN PATTERN TO LAST 6 STS; K6.
ROW 3 (RS): K5; K1 IN ROW BELOW; WORK IN PATTERN TO LAST 6 STS; K1 IN ROW BELOW; K5.

REP ROWS 1-4.

BACK

With 24" US 8, CO 73 (81, 87, 95) STS. WORK IN RIBBING UNTIL PIECE MEASURES 2 (2, 2, 2)" FROM CO EDGE, ENDING WITH RS FACING FOR NEXT ROW. WORK IN FISHERMAN'S RIB UNTIL PIECE MEASURES 17 (17, 18, 18)" FROM CO EDGE.

SHAPE RAGLANS

CONTINUING IN FISHERMAN'S RIB, BO 4 STS AT BEG OF NEXT 2 ROWS. REP THE 4 ROWS OF DECREASE PATTERN 14 (10, 11, 7) TIMES, THEN WORK ONLY ROWS 1 AND 2 OF DECREASE PATTERN 8 (16, 18, 26) TIMES. PLACE REM 21 (21, 21, 21) STS ON HOLDER.

FRONT

WORK SAME AS FOR BACK.

SLEEVES

With 24" US 8, CO 31 (35, 35, 39) STS. WORK IN RIBBING UNTIL PIECE MEASURES 2" FROM CO EDGE, ENDING WITH RS FACING FOR NEXT ROW. WORK IN FISHERMAN'S RIB, **AND AT SAME TIME**, INC 1 ST AT BEG AND END OF EVERY 8TH ROW 15 (15, 16, 16) TIMES. WORK WITHOUT FURTHER SHAPING ON REM 61 (65, 67, 71) STS UNTIL PIECE MEASURES 17 (17, 18, 18)" FROM CO EDGE.

SHAPE RAGLANS

CONTINUING IN FISHERMAN'S RIB, BO 4 STS AT BEG OF NEXT 2 ROWS. REP THE 4 ROWS OF DECREASE PATTERN 16 (13, 16, 14) TIMES, THEN WORK ONLY ROWS 1 AND 2 OF DECREASE PATTERN 4 (9, 7, 11) TIMES.

FINAL DECREASE ROW: K5, SL2TOG, K1, P2SSO, K5.
NEXT ROW (WS): KNIT.

PLACE REM 11 (11, 11, 11) STS ON HOLDER.

NECK

PLACE STS ON HOLDERS ONTO 16" US 8, RS FACING, IN THE FOLLOWING ORDER: BACK, LEFT SLEEVE, FRONT, RIGHT SLEEVE (POINTS OF NEEDLE WILL BE BETWEEN RIGHT SLEEVE AND BACK). MOVE LAST ST OF RIGHT SLEEVE TO LEFT-HAND NEEDLE. JOIN, AND WORK IN THE RND AS FOLLOWS:

NEXT RND: *P2TOG (LAST ST OF RIGHT SLEEVE AND FIRST ST OF BACK), ([K1, P1] TWICE), ([K1 IN ROW BELOW, P1] 5 TIMES), K1 IN ROW BELOW, ([P1, K1] TWICE), P2TOG, ([K1, P1] TWICE), K1 IN ROW BELOW, ([P1, K1] TWICE)**; REP FROM * TO ** ONCE MORE.

WORK IN NECK RIBBING UNTIL NECK MEASURES 1½ (1½, 1½, 1½)". CHANGE TO 16" US 9 AND WORK NECK RIBBING FOR AN ADDITIONAL 1½ (1½, 1½, 1½)". BO LOOSELY IN PATTERN.

FINISHING

SEW SIDE AND SLEEVE SEAMS. WEAVE IN ENDS. BLOCK TO FINISHED MEASUREMENTS.

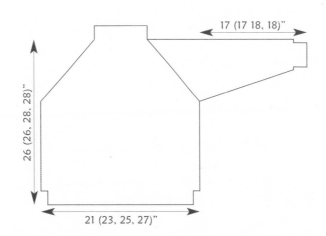

simply scarves

lindy

SCARF

With US 5, CO 53 sts. Reading odd-numbered (RS) rows from right to left and even-numbered (WS) rows from left to right, work Foundation Rows of Chart once, then rep Rows 4-13 until scarf measures approx. 52" from CO edge. BO on Row 13 of Chart.

FINISHING

Weave in ends. Block gently so as not to lose the fluted effect.

MATERIALS

Yarn: Lana Grossa "Cashmere+" - 5 skeins. Shown in #5 and #6.
Needles: US 5 (3.75 mm), *or correct needle to obtain gauge.*

MEASUREMENTS

Width: 8½". Length: 52".

GAUGE

On US 5 in Chart: 25 sts and 26 rows = 4".

CHART

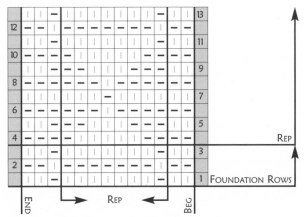

KEY

| | K on right side rows ; P on wrong side rows. |
| − | P on right side rows ; K on wrong side rows. |

claire

SCARF

WITH US 5, CO 54 STS.

ROW 1 (WS): *K1, P1**; REP FROM * TO **.
ROW 2 (RS): *P1, K1**; REP FROM * TO **.
ROW 3 (WS): REP ROW 1.
ROW 4 (RS): REP ROW 2.
ROW 5 (WS): PURL.

ROW 6 (RS): ([K2TOG] 3 TIMES); *([YO, K1] 6 TIMES); ([K2TOG] 6 TIMES)**; REP FROM * TO **; END ([YO, K1] 6 TIMES); ([K2TOG] 3 TIMES).

ROW 7 (WS): PURL.
ROW 8 (RS): KNIT.
ROW 9 (WS): PURL.

REP ROWS 6-9 UNTIL PIECE MEASURES APPROX. 56" FROM CO EDGE. WORK ROWS 6-7. WORK ROWS 2-4. WORK ROW 1. BO IN KNIT.

FINISHING

MAKE TASSELS AND ATTACH TO EACH END OF SCARF WHERE PATTERN CAUSES END TO CURVE OUTWARD. OUR SCARF HAS 4 TASSELS AT ONE END AND 5 TASSELS AT OTHER END. WEAVE IN ENDS. BLOCK TO FINISHED MEASUREMENTS.

MATERIALS
YARN: LANA GROSSA "CASHMERE+" - 5 SKEINS.
SHOWN IN #3.
NEEDLES: US 5 (3.75 MM), *OR CORRECT NEEDLE TO OBTAIN GAUGE.*

MEASUREMENTS
WIDTH: 7¼". LENGTH: 56" (EXCLUDING TASSELS).

GAUGE
ON US 5 IN PATTERN ST: 22 STS AND 30 ROWS = 4".

NOTE: SCARF IS KNITTED IN TWO PIECES, FROM THE CENTER TOWARDS THE POINTS, THEN ARE JOINED TOGETHER. POINTS APPEAR WHEN STS ARE BOUND OFF.

SCARF

1ST PIECE (MAKE 2 TRIANGLES)

1ST TRIANGLE
WITH US 5 AND COLOR A, CO 3 STS AND KNIT 1 ROW.

ROW 1 (RS): WITH COLOR B, KNIT INTO FRONT AND BACK OF FIRST ST; KNIT TO LAST ST; KNIT INTO FRONT AND BACK OF LAST ST.
ROW 2 (WS): WITH COLOR B, KNIT
ROW 3 (RS): WITH COLOR A, KNIT INTO FRONT AND BACK OF FIRST ST; KNIT TO LAST ST; KNIT INTO FRONT AND BACK OF LAST ST.
ROW 4 (WS): WITH COLOR A, KNIT

REP ROWS 1-4 UNTIL THERE ARE 19 STS, ENDING WITH RS FACING FOR NEXT ROW. PLACE STS ON HOLDER.

2ND TRIANGLE
WORK SAME AS FOR **1ST TRIANGLE**, LEAVING STS ON NEEDLE.

JOIN TRIANGLES
WITH RS FACING, PLACE STS OF BOTH TRIANGLES ONTO SAME NEEDLE WITH MARKER BETWEEN THEM, AND CONTINUING TO ALTERNATE COLORS AS SET, WORK AS FOLLOWS:

ROW 1 (RS): KNIT INTO FRONT AND BACK OF FIRST ST; KNIT TO WITHIN 1 ST OF MARKER; SL 2 STS TOG KNITWISE, K1, PASS SL STS OVER; KNIT TO LAST ST; KNIT INTO FRONT AND BACK OF LAST ST (38 STS ON NEEDLE).
ROW 2 (WS): KNIT.

REP ROWS 1 AND 2 UNTIL PIECE MEASURES APPROX 30" FROM CO EDGE. BO ALL STS.

2ND PIECE (MAKE 2 TRIANGLES)

WORK SAME AS FOR **1ST PIECE**, UNTIL WORK MEASURES 2" FROM CO EDGE, THEN OMIT CENTER DOUBLE DEC ON RS ROW. REP THIS STEP TWICE MORE AT 1" INTERVALS (44 STS ON NEEDLE). WORK UNTIL PIECE MEASURES APPROX 30". BO ALL STS.

FINISHING

SEW CO EDGES OF SCARF TOG. IF DESIRED, MAKE POMPONS—2 IN EACH COLOR—AND ATTACH TO POINTS.

jester

MATERIALS

YARN: LANA GROSSA "CASHMERE+" - 3 SKEINS EACH OF COLOR A AND COLOR B. SHOWN IN COLOR A (#12) AND COLOR B (#8), AND IN COLOR A (#9) AND COLOR B (#13).

NEEDLES: US 5 (3.75 MM), *OR CORRECT NEEDLE TO OBTAIN GAUGE.*

MEASUREMENTS

LENGTH: APPROX. 60".

GAUGE

ON US 5 IN GARTER ST: 20 STS AND 40 ROWS = 4".

Abbreviations

ALT = ALTERNATE

BEG = BEGINNING

BO = BIND OFF

CC = CONTRAST COLOR

CN = CABLE NEEDLE

CO = CAST ON

DEC = DECREASE(ING)

GS = GARTER STITCH

INC = INCREASE(ING)

K = KNIT

K1B = KNIT THROUGH BACK LOOP

K2TOG = KNIT 2 STS TOGETHER

K2TOGTBL = KNIT 2 STS TOGETHER THROUGH BACK LOOP

M1 = MAKE 1 ST (INC) - LIFT THE RUNNING THREAD BETWEEN THE
ST JUST WORKED AND THE NEXT ST AND KNIT INTO THE BACK OF THIS LOOP

MC = MAIN COLOR

P = PURL

P2SSO = PASS 2 SLIPPED STS OVER

P2TOG = PURL 2 STS TOGETHER

PATT = PATTERN

PSSO = PASS SLIPPED STITCH OVER ST JUST KNITTED

REM = REMAINING

REP = REPEAT

RND = ROUND

RS = RIGHT SIDE

SL = SLIP

SL1WYIB = WITH YARN IN BACK, SLIP 1 ST PURLWISE

SL1WYIF = WITH YARN IN FRONT, SLIP 1 ST PURLWISE

SSK = SL 2 STS (ONE AT A TIME) KNITWISE; WITH LEFT-HAND
NEEDLE, KNIT THESE TWO STS TOG THROUGH FRONT OF STS

ST(S) = STITCH(ES)

ST ST = STOCKINETTE STITCH

TBL = THROUGH BACK LOOP

TOG = TOGETHER

WS = WRONG SIDE

YB (YARN BACK) = TAKE YARN TO BACK OF WORK

YF (YARN FORWARD) = BRING YARN TO FRONT OF WORK

YO = YARN OVER NEEDLE

A selection of Lana Grossa yarns can be found at these fine stores:

ALABAMA
Huntsville - Yarn Expressions
800-283-8409

ALASKA
Anchorage - LANA GROSSA AT Knitting Frenzy
800-478-8322
Fairbanks - LANA GROSSA AT Knitting Frenzy
907-488-8005

ARKANSAS
Little Rock - LANA GROSSA AT The Handworks Gallery
501-664-6300

CALIFORNIA
Alameda - Yarn!
510-749-8319
Campbell - Rug & Yarn Hut
408-871-0411
El Cerrito - Skein Lane
510-525-1828
Los Altos - LANA GROSSA AT Uncommon Threads
650-941-1815
Los Angeles - LANA GROSSA AT Knit Cafe
323-658-5648
Mendocino - Mendocino Yarn Shop
707-937-0921
Menlo Park - LANA GROSSA AT The Knitter's Studio
650-322-9200
Mill Valley - Yarn Collection
415-383-9276
Oakland - LANA GROSSA AT Article Pract
510-652-7435
Oakland - Knitting Basket
800-654-4887
Pacific Grove - LANA GROSSA AT Monarch Knitting & Quilts
831-647-9276
Rocklin - Filati
800-398-9043
San Carlos - Creative Hands
650-591-0588
San Francisco - Greenwich Yarns
415-567-2535
San Francisco - LANA GROSSA AT ImagiKnit
415-621-6642
San Francisco - Urban Knitting Studio
415-552-5333
San Leandro - Creative Accents
510-383-9003
San Jose - Knitting Room
408-264-7229
Saratoga - The Braid Box Knitting Studio
408-867-5010
Sebastopol - Knitting Workshop
707-824-0699
Sherman Oaks - Needle World
818-784-2442
Studio City - La Knitterie Parisienne
800-228-9927
Ukiah - Heidi's Yarn Haven
707-462-0544
West Hills - A Yarn For All Seasons
818-999-2720

CONNECTICUT
Avon - Wool Connection
800-933-9665

GEORGIA
Roswell - Cast-On Cottage
888-998-9019

ILLINOIS
Chicago - We'll Keep You In Stitches
312-642-2540
Lake Forest - Keweenaw Shepherd
847-295-9524
Northbrook - 3 Bags Full
847-361-8616

INDIANA
Fort Wayne - Cass Street Depot
888-420-2292
Indianapolis - Mass Ave Knit Shop
800-675-8565

MAINE
Camden - Stitchery Square
207-236-9773

MARYLAND
Annapolis - Yarn Garden
410-224-2033
Ashton - Fiberworks
301-774-9031
Baltimore - Woolworks
410-337-9030
Bethesda - Yarns International
800-927-6728
Glyndon - Woolstock
410-517-1020

MASSACHUSETTS
Boston - Windsor Button
617-482-4969
Cambridge - Woolcott & Co.
617-547-2837
Lenox - Colorful Stitches
800-413-6111
Lexington - LANA GROSSA AT Wild & Woolly Studio
781-861-7717

MICHIGAN
Ada - LANA GROSSA AT Clever Ewe
Birmingham - Knitting Room
248-540-3623
Macomb - Crafty Lady
586-566-8008
Marquette - Town Folk Gallery
906-225-9010
Plymouth - Old Village Yarn
734-451-0580
Rochester - LANA GROSSA AT Skeins on Main
248-656-9300

MINNESOTA
Excelsior - Coldwater Collaborative
952-401-7501
Minneapolis - Clickity Sticks - Yarns & Such
612-724-2500

Minneapolis - Clickity Sticks - Yarns & Such
612-724-2500
Minneapolis - Linden Hill Yarns
612-929-1255
Minneapolis - LANA GROSSA AT Needlework Unlimited
888-936-2454
Osseo - Amazing Threads
763-391-7700
St. Paul - LANA GROSSA AT Three Kittens Yarn Shop
651-457-4969
St. Paul - LANA GROSSA AT The Yarnery
651-222-5793
White Bear Lake - LANA GROSSA AT A Sheepy Yarn Shoppe
800-480-5462

NEW HAMPSHIRE
Exeter - Charlotte's Web
603-778-1417
Laconia - The Yarn Shop & Fibers
603-528-1221

NEW JERSEY
Lambertville - LANA GROSSA AT Simply Knit
609-397-7101

NEW YORK
Fayetteville - Village Yarns
315-637-0416
Rochester - Village Yarn Shop
585-454-6064

NORTH CAROLINA
Black Mountain - Naked Sheep Yarn Shop
828-669-0600
Greensboro - Yarns, Etc.
336-370-1233
Huntersville - Knit One, Stitch Too
704-655-9558
Raleigh - LANA GROSSA AT Great Yarns
800-810-0045

OHIO
Columbus - Wolfe Fiber Arts
614-487-9980
Mansfield - Bumble Bee Yarns
419-525-1110
Rocky River - River Color Studio
440-333-9276
Toledo - Fiberworks Knitting
419-389-1821

OREGON
Ashland - LANA GROSSA AT Web-sters
800-482-9801
Bandon - The Wool Company
541-347-3912
Portland - Northwest Wools
503-244-5024
Portland - LANA GROSSA AT Yarn Garden
503-239-7950

PENNSYLVANIA
Chadd's Ford - Garden of Yarn
610-459-5599
Chambersburg - The Yarn Basket
717-263-3236
Duncansville - Victoria's Needlework
800-574-2033
Lancaster - LANA GROSSA AT Oh Susanna Yarns
717-393-5146
Monroeville - Bonnie Knits
412-856-7033
Philadelphia - Rosie's Yarn Cellar
215-977-9276
Philadelphia - LANA GROSSA AT Tangled Web
215-242-1271
West Reading - LANA GROSSA AT Yarn Gallery
613-373-1622
Willow Street - Legacy Yarn
717-464-7575

RHODE ISLAND
Providence - LANA GROSSA AT A Stitch Above
401-455-0269

TENNESSEE
Chattanooga - Genuine Pearl
423-267-7335

TEXAS
Austin - Hill Country Weavers
512-707-7396
San Antonio - Yarn Barn of San Antonio
210-826-3679

VIRGINIA
Alexandria - Springwater Workshop
703-549-3634
Charlottesville - It's a Stitch
434-973-0331
Falls Church - Aylin's Woolgatherer
703-573-1900
Midlothian - Got Yarn
800-594-0323
Richmond - Knitting Basket
804-282-2909

WASHINGTON
Bainbridge Island - Churchmouse Yarns & Teas
206-780-2686
Seattle - Hilltop Yarn & Needlepoint
206-282-1332
Seattle - The Weaving Works
888-524-1221
Tacoma - Fibers, Etc.
253-531-3257

WISCONSIN
Appleton - Jane's Knitting Hutch
920-954-9001
Delafield - LANA GROSSA AT Knitting Ark
920-787-1686
Middleton - Coyote Yarns
608-236-0270
Milwaukee - LANA GROSSA AT Ruhama's Yarn & Needlepoint
608-236-0270

"LANA GROSSA AT . . ." stores carry a wide range of Lana Grossa yarns.

Editorial Director   **David Codling**

Pattern Editor & Graphic Design   **Gregory Courtney**

Technical Editor   **Diane Brown**

Designers   **Carol Lapin, Nadine Shapiro, Sandi Rosner, Joe Wilcox, Diane Brown & Janis Fang**

Photography   **Kathryn Martin & Nancy Denkin**

Garments Modeled by   **Michelle Rich**

Makeup & Hair Styling   **Kira Lee**

Clothing Stylist   **Betsy Westman**

Buttons   **Muench Buttons**

Color Reproduction & Printing   **Global Interprint, Inc.**

Published and Distributed By   **Unicorn Books and Crafts, Inc.**

Printed in Hong Kong

ISBN
1-893063-06-2

1 2 3 4 5 6 7 8 9 10